In With Flynn
The Boss Behind the President

In With Flynn
The Boss Behind the President

Malcolm MacKay

Brick Tower Press
New York

Brick Tower Press
Manhanset House
Dering Harbor, New York 11965-0342
bricktower@aol.com
The Brick Tower Press colophon is a registered trademark of
J. T. Colby & Company, Inc.
www.IngramContent.com
For sales in the UK and Europe, stef@gazellebooks.co.uk

Library of Congress Cataloging-in-Publication Data
MacKay, Malcolm
In With Flynn
The Boss Behind the President
Includes biographical references and footnotes
ISBN 978-1-899694-88-4

1. Flynn, Ed— 2. Politics—United States 3. Biography—Political
Leaders 4. Business—New York

Copyright © 2020 by Malcolm MacKay
Trade Paper, Nonfiction

First Printing, September 2020

Ed Flynn, the political boss of the Bronx for over thirty years, provided crucial support to Franklin Roosevelt over and over again. Personally honest, competent and public spirited, he also hand-picked candidates—particularly for the higher level positions—who were known for being the same. His control of Bronx politics was virtually absolute: his candidates never lost an election. He served as national party chairman in the early 1940s and in 1944 literally put Harry Truman on the ticket as FDR's running mate. The president and the boss, so different in so many ways, became close personal friends.

Front cover photograh: Newlyweds Helen and Ed Flynn leaving St. Jerome's in Mott Haven, 1927.

PREVIOUS BOOKS

The Rise and Fall of Richard Whitney

ACKNOWLEDGMENTS

While I am grateful to many people who assisted me in writing this book, I would like to mention several specifically. My wife Julia was a constant source of encouragement, not to mention spelling. Four good friends, all Brooklyn neighbors, carefully reviewed drafts: Sara Faison, Bob Whiteford, Craig Whitney and Warren Weshchler. Ed Flynn's children Sheila Flynn DeCosse and Dick Flynn provided photographs, written materials and recollections that were invaluable. Shirley Freni turned my handwriting into type others could read. Finally there is John Colby, always so supportive, who was willing to step forward for a second time as my publisher.

Table of Contents

TIME

THE WEEKLY NEWSMAGAZINE

CHAIRMAN OF DEMOCRATIC NATIONAL COMMITTEE

Flynn on *Time* magazine's cover in 1942.

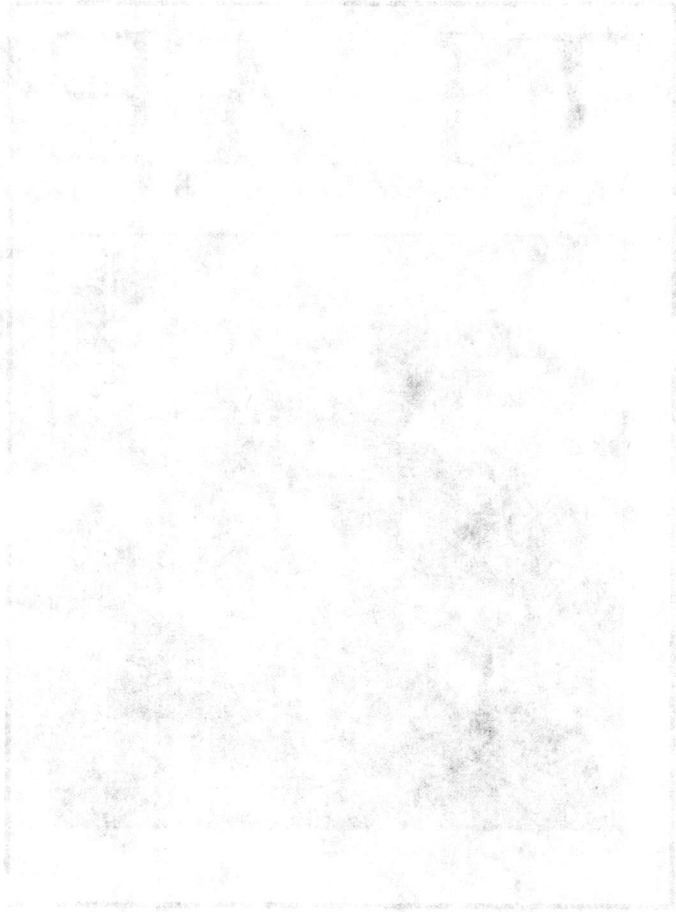

FOREWORD

There was a time not so long ago when political bosses—perhaps particularly the chairmen of the urban Democratic organizations (or machines)—selected the party's nominees from top to bottom of the ballot. This was true for elections in a given machine's locale, as well as nationally when the bosses came together behind a candidate. As late as 1968, Hubert Humphrey, with strong machine and union backing, received the Democratic presidential nomination without entering, much less winning, a single primary.

Today, at least at the top of the ticket, money and the media allow candidates to by-pass the regular organization and appeal directly to the voters. It is the age of the political entrepreneur and pressure group. Donald Trump ran against his party and yet won its nomination. More democratic? Perhaps, but at a price.

What follows is the story of an old-time political boss, Edward J. Flynn of the Bronx. Much of the narrative revolves around his relationship with one of America's most successful politicians, Franklin D. Roosevelt. Both men lived in a world where winning elections was imperative and compromises were made, yet both men were in the political game for reasons greater than winning itself. Noted theologian Reinhold Niebuhr caught the connection between politics and purpose when he wrote that there was no reason "to believe Abraham Lincoln, the statesman and opportunist, was morally inferior to William Lloyd Garrison, the prophet. The moral achievement of statesmen must be judged in terms which take account of the limitations of human society which the statesman must, and the prophet need not, consider."

Ed Flynn was a practical man in the real world. One of his sons said his father made decisions with "a hard head." But a closer look reveals something else—a steady push to move men, events and policy toward better ends.

INTRODUCTION

President Franklin Roosevelt died in Warm Springs, Georgia, on April 12, 1945, 18 days before Hitler's suicide and four months before the Japanese surrender. He was 63 and only two months into his fourth term, during which he hoped to create a new and peaceful world order.

Less than three hours later—7:09 pm—the chief justice administered the oath of office to Vice President Harry S Truman in the west wing of the White House. Earlier Truman had expressed his sorrow to the late president's widow, asking if there was anything he could do for her. "Is there anything we can do for you?" Eleanor Roosevelt replied. "For you are the one in trouble now."

The new president, according to one report, was "absolutely dazed" by the day's events. He went back to his apartment, where a neighbor's wife provided him with a turkey sandwich and a glass of milk. The next day he asked to meet with four men. One was Harry Hopkins, Roosevelt's most important domestic and foreign policy aide. Another was James F. Byrnes, soon to become the secretary of state, who informed the new president of the existence of the atomic bomb. A third was Admiral William Leahy, the late president's chief of staff. The fourth was Ed Flynn, whose only title was boss of the Bronx. Flynn's inclusion in the four did not surprise White House reporters. One described him as "the most powerful political leader in the country." Another wrote that he was also "the most quiet." Both Roosevelt and Truman owed their presidencies to Flynn.

Historians have focused on Louis Howe and the previously mentioned Harry Hopkins as Roosevelt's closest advisors. Howe came first, an Albany reporter who devoted his life to FDR's ascendancy to the White House. Howe died in 1936, but by then there was Hopkins, the social worker turned government administrator who handled a myriad of domestic and foreign assignments. Flynn never minded his low profile because he believed that, to be successful, a political boss had to avoid center stage.

The facts are, however, that, for the last 25 years of Roosevelt's life, Flynn gave him loyal and, at times, crucial political support, unvarnished policy advice and genuine friendship. During this time Flynn ran the most successful political machine in the country. Standing alone, the Bronx would have been America's sixth largest city, and it was not unusual to have 85 percent of those eligible actually vote. Candidates who were "in with Flynn" invariably succeeded, which is how some etymologists believe the expression originated.

Around the White House, Flynn was known for being direct and honest. He was not afraid to show his anger, or what he called his "Irish." He believed in an inclusive society and strongly supported civil and labor rights. He shared Roosevelt's desire for reasonable accommodations with the Soviet Union after the war, and strenuously opposed the red scare tactics of postwar militant anti-communism. Although not personally as close to Truman as he was to Roosevelt, Flynn put Truman on the ticket in 1944 and played a significant national leadership role in the late 1940s. He died, still in the saddle as the boss of the Bronx, in 1953.

1 IRELAND

The road to understanding Ed Flynn and practically all the other Democratic bosses of his time begins in Ireland, an island the size of Indiana with a population never more than eight million. The Flynns came from County Cork, in and around Ballinspittle, or town of the hospital. The land, along the coast southeast of Dublin, is relatively flat and famously fertile. Cork, long known as "the rebel county," has a history of failed uprisings against various invaders and overlords. The defeat of the Irish at Kinsale, County Cork, in 1601 led to English control of the entire island by the end of the 17th century. The English feared, after Henry VIII's break with Rome, that Ireland could become a launching site for the counter-reformation. In fact, at various times Spanish and French troops did assemble on Irish soil with the encouragement of the Catholic underclass—90 percent or more of the entire population—but to little avail.

Anglican gentry were installed as land owners. The land was often managed by local agents who remitted rental income to absentee landlords living in England. The Irish worked the land as tenants at will without the protection of written leases, and thus were subject to immediate subdivision and foreclosure. The English (and then British) government encouraged the migrations of Scot Presbyterians to Ireland, creating conditions for 400 years of bloody conflict.

Colonial practices were codified in the Penal Laws of 1695 banning Catholics from purchasing land, voting and holding public office. Catholicism itself was strictly proscribed and Catholic education outlawed. It is no wonder that, as Cecil Woodham-Smith observed in *The Great Hunger*, Irish children grew up with such heroes as Philip of Spain, James II and Napoleon, while their English counterparts preferred Elizabeth, William III and Wellington. Napoleon gave support to the rebellion of 1798, and Germany delighted in the famous Easter 1916 uprising, occurring in the middle of World War I.

Rural Ireland may have been the poorest place in Europe in the early 1800s. Then things got worse. In the autumn of 1845, a potato blight struck, turning the island's most important crop "black and slimy in a matter of hours," as reported in a New York paper. The potato famine lasted until 1852, leaving one million dead while another two million emigrated to the United States and elsewhere. The ruling British authorities worried that government welfare "to the undeserving" would weaken the Irish people, encouraging "despondency and idleness." They also insisted that the export of beef and non-potato agricultural products continue despite mass starvation at home.

The refusal of the British authorities to deal appropriately with the famine's consequences magnified the long-held Irish sense of powerlessness and resentment. Just before he died in 1847, the Irish patriot Daniel O'Connell, the first Catholic member of the British parliament since the Reformation, told the House of Commons: "Ireland is in your power. If you do not save her, she cannot save herself." Another Irish nationalist, John Mitchel, put it more directly, "The Almighty, indeed, sent the potato blight, but the English created the famine."

Survivors of the famine, whether they remained in Ireland or emigrated, came away from the experience with a commitment to rectify their people's historic powerlessness. As Terry Golway wrote in *Machine Made*, "But there is no question that a bumper crop of bitterness and rage was harvested from the island's blackened potato fields. Famine survivors absorbed a new and fundamental lesson about power. Those who possess it will never be helpless, and those who are denied it are doomed to starvation and exile when resources become scarce."

Ed Flynn's children believe their Flynn ancestors were mostly tenant farmers in the vicinity of Ballinspittle. They may have been a bit better off financially than most, as indicated by Ed's father Henry having attended Trinity College, the ancient Anglican college in Dublin that first admitted Catholic men in 1793. Interestingly the Irish Catholic Church actively discouraged—even by excommunication—its young men from attending Trinity for fear that they might be enticed to leave the faith.

As the 19th century progressed, Irish Catholics gained political rights and economic power. The Catholic Relief Act of 1829 abolished formal legal discrimination against Catholics. Gradually public education developed, but, as with Trinity College, the Catholic hierarchy found the instruction too English and Anglican. Catholics wanted their own parochial schools, a desire that crossed the Atlantic with the immigrants. It wasn't until the Wyndham Land Purchase Act of 1903 that the British government created a process to break up the large estates and devolve land ownership to the tenants. Flynn's children remember their father buying a tractor for the Irish relatives.

Newlyweds Helen and Ed Flynn leaving St.
Jerome's in Mott Haven, 1927.

2 AMERICA

In the 1840s, roughly half of all immigrants were Irish, and they crowded together in such places as New York's Five Points on the lower East Side. According to historian Kevin Kenny, "The Irish poor lived in basements, cellars, and one-room apartments lacking natural light and ventilation and frequently flooded with sewage. They suffered from alarmingly high rates of cholera, yellow fever, typhus, tuberculosis, and pneumonia. They also succumbed to mental illness, often complicated by alcohol abuse." Although most spoke English, they were otherwise unprepared to succeed in their new environment.

The Irish were resented by the older American families. The "know-nothing" political movement was a reaction to mid-century immigration with its core belief that Catholicism was incompatible with democracy and loyalty to America. The Irish were often portrayed as unruly, dishonest, lazy and prone to drink. In the 1850s in New York City, considerably more than half those arrested by the police were of Irish origin. The unfortunate were carted to jail in "paddy wagons." During the draft riots in the summer of 1863, Irish immigrants took out their revenge on another group competing for unskilled employment, free blacks.

We think of ethnic, racial and religious hostility as the curse of the less secure and educated, but prejudice against immigrants, and perhaps particularly the Irish, easily jumped class barriers. Henry Adams, a highly distinguished literary figure and the grandson and great grandson of presidents, complained of "the particular Irish maggot rather lower than the Jew, but with more or less the same appetite for cheese." Many were the townhouse in need of maid service that displayed the window sign: *Irish need not apply*. Some of the loudest anti-immigrant voices belonged to abolitionists, a fact noted in the Irish community.

The Irish brought to America the values and attitudes of the old country. They were insular and intensely loyal to members of their own group, and ever watchful for traitors within. As is common with a subjugated people, there was a certain tolerance for rule breaking. Religion was an integral part of their identity, and the Irish came to control the American Catholic Church. The post-famine Irish Americans were united in their beliefs that:

> •their children should be educated in parochial schools that receive public funding;
> •Sundays are for recreation as well as worship;
> •men have a right to their whiskey;
> •the government should help the destitute whatever the cause of an individual's need; and
> •you can't trust the English, or Americans who are like them.

There was one place in their new country where the Irish were welcome: the Democratic parties in most of the cities. The urban political machines offered desperately needed assistance—jobs and other help—to the arriving immigrants in return for votes. As Terry Golway put it, "Every time they [the machine] found a job for an unemployed immigrant, every time they arranged for a delivery of coal to a struggling widow, they did more than win a vote. Wittingly or not, they challenged the transatlantic Anglo-Protestant culture of rugged individualism and minimalist government."

Just as there is today, there was considerable nativist resistance to granting immigrants the right to vote. Walt Whitman, for example, complained of the "appalling dangers of universal suffrage," and a movement developed to restrict the obtaining of citizenship. It was, however, to no avail. Soon the Irish took over the urban machines, embracing what the late Senator Daniel Patrick Moynihan called "the possibility of politics."

It didn't take long for the political machines to take on characteristics of the Catholic Church. Both church and party operated through a central hierarchy. One had cardinals, bishops and local priests, and the other county chairmen or bosses, assembly district leaders and election and ward captains. Like churches, politically connected saloons and local club houses were places for community gatherings. Elected officials and holders of patronage jobs were expected to contribute to the party's treasury. The creation and extension of civil service, very much an important goal of reform-minded old America, was an anathema to the political machines. Like the church, the machines provided help to the needy without the recipients being subjected to tests of personal worthiness.

City political machines developed—deservedly—reputations for corruption. As a British ambassador to the United States put it, "There is no denying that the government of the cities is the one conspicuous failure of the United States." Nowhere was this more true than with Tammany Hall, the regular Democratic organization in Manhattan from the time of Aaron Burr. One historian described Tammany bosses such as William Tweed and

Richard Croker as "sleazy, unprincipled crooks dedicated to plundering the public treasury."

Tammany men and their counterparts in other cities (and the growing outer counties of New York City) grew rich on bribes from contractors and proprietors of saloons, brothels and gambling dens. According to Tweed biographer Kenneth Balkerman, "It's hard not to admire the skills behind Tweed's system … The Tweed ring at its height was an engineering marvel, strong and solid, strategically deployed to control key power points, the courts, the legislature, the treasury and the ballot box. Its frauds had a great grandeur of scale and an elegance of structure, money laundering, profit sharing and organization."

Nobody captured the mindset of a Tammany operative better than George Washington Plunkett, a member of the party's old guard in the late 19th century:

• "The men who put through the primary law are the same crowd that stands for the civil service blight and they have the same objects in view—the destruction of government by party, the downfall of the constitution and hell generally."

• "This civil service law is the biggest fraud of the age. It is the curse of the nation. There can't be no real patriotism while it lasts. How are you goin' to interest our young men in this country if you have no offices to give them when they work for their party?"

• on reformers: "They were mornin' glories—looked lovely in the mornin' and withered up in a short time, while the regular machines went on flourishin' forever, like fine old oaks."

• "The politicians who make a lastin' success in politics are the men who are always loyal to their friends, even up to the gate of the State prison, if necessary." and

• in discussing the educational level of the Tammany district leaders: "Of course, we ain't all bookworms and college professors. If we were, Tammany might win an election once in four thousand years."

3 THE BRONX

"The Bronx? No thonx," wrote Ogden Nash, reflecting on a common view that you wouldn't want to live there. How different the perspective of Jonas Bronck, who in 1639 became the first European landowner: "It is a veritable paradise and needs but the industrious hand of man to make it the finest and most beautiful region in all the world."

North of the Harlem River, the Bronx remained farmland, with a few scattered villages, for 250 years. After several annexations by New York City in the 19th century, it became one of the city's five counties in 1914. Its population, only 37,400 in 1870 and up to 100,000 by 1890, doubled in the next 10 years. By 1930, it was 1.3 million, making it—were it an independent city—larger than St. Louis, Baltimore and Boston. This extraordinary growth was driven by the extensions of the elevated train and subway lines from Manhattan. The Third Avenue El crossed the Harlem River in 1888, and by 1900 extended far north. In 1904, the first subway connected the Bronx and Manhattan.

These transportation advances allowed working-class families in Manhattan to seek better living conditions in the Bronx. Five- and six-story rental apartment buildings sprouted up by the thousands, offering amenities beyond tenants' dreams. Leon Trotsky, living in the Bronx in 1917 before going back to Russia to help lead the revolution, noted, "The apartment, at $18 a month, was equipped with all sorts of conveniences that we Europeans were quite unused to, electric lights, gas cooking range, bath, telephone, automatic service elevator and even a chute for the garbage."

According to the 1930 census, 70 percent of Bronx residents were foreign born or first-generation natives. Half were of Eastern European Jewish origin. They were not wealthy, but most were financially self-sustaining. As Senator Moynihan noted, "In the Great Depression of the 1930s, the Bronx was called 'the city without a slum.' It had the lowest unemployment rate of any of the five counties of New York, and ... was during this period one of the few areas of the country that experienced privately financed residential construction."

Henry Flynn, Ed's father, was born in County Cork in 1854. College educated, he wasn't your typical Irish immigrant when he arrived with his wife Sarah Mallen Flynn in 1870. They appear to have settled directly in the Mott Haven area of the South Bronx, buying a small house on Willis Avenue. Mott Haven was really a village, and Ed remembered his father describing neighborhood farms. The newcomers, predominately but not entirely Irish Catholics, were a bit more prosperous than those in the tenements of the lower East Side. According to Ed, "The people who came to settle in the Bronx were mostly immigrants who were of a better type. They were men and women who wished to bring their families up in an atmosphere away from the activities of a large city."

As best his grandchildren understand, Henry spent his entire career "in unexciting positions" at the New York Central Rail Road. Ed described his father as "a dignified, cultured man. I remember well that he never seemed to care for money, or for any of the other furnishings or marks of material success. Looking back, I can see now that he simply never allowed himself to be ruled and broken by the necessity of earning a living."

Sarah, as Ed would recall, "ruled" the brood of five children, "a kindly yet immensely practical woman whose capacity for planning kept the household together and accounted for most of the educational opportunities that came to her children." It was Sarah, seeing the possibilities in Bronx real estate, who saved what she could to buy land. This was a smart move. As an article in *The New Yorker* noted about the Bronx at the turn of the 20th century, "Lots leaped from five hundred dollars to five thousand dollars literally overnight." It was thanks to Sarah's investments that the family, particularly relative to its community, became wealthy. Of the children, the oldest, Fred, became a beloved local doctor, and a sister a public school principal. Ed, the youngest, was born in 1891.

4 YOUNG MAN

"A playboy" with "hundreds of warm friends" is how Ed Flynn described his young self. Skipping college, he went directly from Fordham Prep to Fordham Law School, graduating with honors at age 20 in 1912. (In 1925, he would also be awarded an honorary degree.) Admitted to the bar at age 21, he began a local law practice with a neighborhood friend, Bill McKeown, who was famous in the community for his baseball skills. McKeown, pitching for Fordham, had beaten the New York Giants, two to one, in an exhibition game. The new firm's prospects were good.

Just as he was born a Catholic, Flynn was born a Democrat. His father Henry didn't need the party's patronage, but he was a Democrat, according to Ed, "because he sensed that, for all its Tweeds and Crokers [two corrupt Tammany Hall bosses], the party was, in New York as in the nation, the party of the common man." In 1917 the Democratic leader of the second assembly district in the Bronx, which included Mott Haven, was worried about a challenge to his leadership and needed to field a strong candidate for the vacant assembly seat. The leader, a Flynn family friend, approached Ed about becoming the regular organization candidate. Flynn was only 25 and had never participated in any political activity. In fact, he hadn't even voted. He knew at the time that, while becoming an assemblyman "would do me no harm," nevertheless it "was not the sort of thing to which I wished to dedicate my life."

Why was Flynn chosen? The man himself had no illusions: "I am certain that Brown [the district leader] selected me, not because of anything I stood for, nor because of any personal strength he thought I might bring to the party, but because of my father's good name and Fred's wide acquaintances and high standing in the district."

The young candidate easily won the primary against a rare party insurgent and the election against a Republican sacrificial lamb, the only kind of GOP candidate in the Bronx. Flynn soon learned that, as the Republicans controlled the assembly, "the introduction of bills by Democrats became an empty gesture." He also learned, and accepted, another Albany lesson, "A member followed the lead of his party."

What Flynn did in Albany was make friends, particularly among his fellow Democrats. The party's assembly leader was Jimmy Walker, later the high-living New York mayor also known as Beau James. An assemblyman from Rockland County, Jim Farley, would work closely with Flynn in future years and both would serve as national Democratic chairman. Alfred Smith became governor during Flynn's time in the assembly, and they became allies during the 1920s, only to draw apart when Flynn supported Roosevelt over Smith for president in 1932.

While serving as a young assemblyman, Flynn did have one unpleasant experience with Governor Smith that he would recount years later. Believing in "alleviating the monotony of our residence in Albany with social relaxation," Flynn would go out drinking with Smith's nephew, and word of these "escapades" got back to the governor. One day Flynn was summoned to the executive office, and given "as stiff a dressing down as I have ever gotten." Smith ended the meeting with the prophecy, according to Flynn, that "no good would ever come, either to his nephew or to myself." Flynn "determined then and there to surprise him."

Elected by ever increasing margins to four one-year terms, Flynn was popular with his constituents. The Citizens Union of New York, still today an active good government watchdog, had a somewhat different view. After his first year in the assembly, CU described Flynn as "not particularly attentive or effective … absent on important roll calls … unsatisfactory record of votes." Before Flynn's fourth and final election in 1921, CU was somewhat more positive, "Edward J. Flynn, Democrat, Second District, Record of votes and other activities considerably improved, but, as in former years, often unrecorded." One vote that may have caused CU to be more charitable toward Flynn was in support, despite strong countervailing pressure, of the right of a duly elected assemblyman—albeit a socialist—to serve.

As Flynn would remember 30 years later, there was a back story to the Citizens Union evaluations. When he first ran for the assembly, CU sent him a long candidates' questionnaire, as is still its practice. Flynn described his response: "As I had chatted with hundreds of persons in the old neighborhood during the campaign, and as none of them had raised the questions posed by the Union, I began to wonder in just what way the Union represented the people I was supposed to represent. So I replied to the letter, stating that if they would give me the names of twenty legal residents of my district who were bonafide members of the Citizens Union, I would be happy to answer their questions. I never received a reply to that letter."

During his four years in Albany, Flynn maintained an active law practice. He also speculated successfully in local real estate, often with his mother. While still in his twenties, he later wrote, "I found myself in a comfortable financial position. So

I decided that four years in the Assembly were enough. Political life had no great lure for me. I felt I was wasting my time in Albany." He told the party district leader that he wanted out. He must have thought that his life in politics was over. As he learned almost immediately, he was wrong.

5 SHERIFF OF THE BRONX

As Flynn observed, "Getting out of politics is seldom that easy." As soon as he told his district leader that he wished 1921 to be his last year in the assembly, the Bronx county party chairman or boss, Arthur Murphy, approached him about being the party's citywide candidate for president of the board of aldermen, second only to the mayor in importance. The party leaders in the other counties, however, refused to give this plum to the Bronx and the idea of Flynn's candidacy died. As he recalled, "I suppose I should have been broken-hearted. I was not. Indeed, the feeling that swept over me can best be described as one of genuine relief."

Bronx boss Arthur Murphy, however, had another position for the 29-year-old retiring assemblyman. A rival to the regular organization had declared his candidacy for the job of sheriff, and Murphy needed an attractive candidate, loyal to the party, to run in the primary and protect the regulars' interests. Flynn knew why he was selected, "I had only the record of my four years in the Assembly which ... were not outstanding. My major strength lay with the organization. I had the consolation of knowing that this primary fight involved more than my fortunes." After what he called "an internecine struggle of epic proportions," Flynn succeeded in both the primary and the election. As sheriff, he had to give up his private law practice.

Why become sheriff? With one exception, there wasn't much to the office. It operated two jails—one for adults and one for children—and, for fees, served writs and other court papers involving civil actions. Later, under Mayor LaGuardia and with Flynn's support, the offices in the counties were consolidated into one citywide entity.

The one exception to the irrelevance of the sheriff's office was its importance as a major source of political patronage. It was a place where the "spoils system" remained, despite the efforts of reformers such as Carl Schurz and Theodore Roosevelt to extend hiring and promotions by civil service examinations to most government functions. The Bronx sheriff controlled 62 staff positions (out of a total of 67) that were "exempt" from civil service with its merit-based selection. In fact, the office was the single largest source of exempt positions in the county, except perhaps for federal jobs during the New Deal. Flynn described the exempt positions as "political plums within the gift of the sheriff." He once calculated that as party boss he had influence over 142 exempt jobs in the Bronx, with the sheriff's office responsible for about half of these positions. Loyalty to the organization is an absolute requirement of the patronage system, something Flynn always accepted. As one of his first acts as sheriff, he fired five or six employees who supported his primary opponent. "I could not have in my organizations," he wrote, "anyone who was not interested wholeheartedly in making the administration of my office a success."

Only twice in Flynn's career was there any hint of scandal, each time unjustified. The first was when, as the new sheriff, he followed the usual practice of appointing "honorary deputies." These appointees had no duties and received no pay, but they got to wear a badge, carry a gun and avoid jury duty. The nominees for the position came through the political organizations and their qualifications were never examined. Through the normal process, a man named Arthur

Flegenheimer was suggested to Flynn, and, although he had never heard of Mr. Flegenheimer, he made him an honorary deputy. Later it became known, and covered in the press, that the gentleman was also known as "Dutch Schultz," a notorious bootlegger and a rackets boss. When Flynn stepped down as sheriff in 1925 to practice law with his friend Monroe Goldwater, his successor followed his advice to discontinue the appointment of honorary deputies. Schultz, years later, was killed by a rival mob boss, Lucky Luciano.

6 ANOINTED

Shortly after Flynn became sheriff in January1922, Arthur Murphy, the Bronx Democratic boss who obviously thought so highly of him, died unexpectedly. The party's executive committee, consisting mostly of the captains (or leaders) of the various assembly districts, had the formal authority to choose Murphy's successor. Flynn gave his support, which was particularly valuable as several district captains worked in the sheriff's office, to his local captain, one of several loyal party men who wanted the job.

While Flynn's endorsement was valuable, it was not conclusive. Several candidates continued to compete, with no one achieving a voting majority. In Flynn's description, "This situation continued for some time, and ultimately reached truly alarming proportions. The time seemed to have arrived when only intervention from outside might restore order in the Bronx."

At this point, Flynn received an invitation to meet with Charles Francis Murphy, the boss of bosses as head of Tammany Hall, the Democratic organization in Manhattan. Murphy, although he never held elective office, was the most powerful political leader in the state, and perhaps the entire country. The two men met twice within a few days at Tammany Hall itself, where Flynn had never been. The meetings did not seem to Flynn to go well, as he was committed to his own district leader and would not discuss the possibility of supporting another candidate.

Something about Flynn must have impressed Murphy, however, because a week or so after the second meeting he was called back for a third. This time Murphy informed him that, although as the Manhattan Democratic chairman he had no formal authority over the party's Bronx executive committee, nevertheless he would support a triumvirate to run things in the county. Two members would be assembly district captains currently competing for the job, although not Flynn's district leader, and the third would be Flynn. "This was one of the greatest shocks I have ever received," Flynn later recalled. Before he accepted, he made a point of getting buy-in from his own district captain.

For about three months, the triumvirate tried to function, meeting three times a week in the Bronx and traveling weekly by funeral-home limousine to Murphy's house on East Eighteenth Street. As Flynn remembered their visits, "We would be ushered into his overly elegant parlor ... After an appropriate pause Mr. Murphy would enter and, with great solemnity, say, 'How are you, Stan?' 'How are you, Tom?' And then to me, 'How are you, young man?' Then he would seat himself with his usual dignity and ask, 'How are conditions in the Bronx?' Each of us in turn would reply, 'Excellent.' This would conclude the conference. We would rise, get our hats, climb back into the funeral hack, and proceed solemnly back to the Bronx."

Actually, things were not so good. The triumvirate couldn't work together. The Bronx was losing patronage opportunities and the chance to influence legislation. There was growing support within the county executive committee to elect Flynn chairman, but the other candidates kept throwing up procedural barriers to an actual vote. Flynn met with Murphy privately, vetting his frustrations. Murphy's reply, "There will be a meeting of the [executive] committee tomorrow, and you will be elected chairman."

The next day that is exactly what happened. As Flynn later wrote, "What Mr. Murphy did to bring this about, and to whom he talked, I do not know ... his power was so great that when he gave what is known in politics as 'the word,' opposition crumbled away."

7 MENTOR MURPHY

While technically Manhattan bound, Tammany Hall dominated the entire city's political life until well into the 20th century. Charles Murphy, a rather austere saloon keeper, led Tammany from 1902 until his death in 1924. He succeeded Richard Croker as Tammany boss, Croker having made a quick departure for England and eventually Ireland with several million ill-gotten dollars.

Reformers were skeptical when Murphy took over. Even a decade later an upstate Democratic state senator, Franklin D. Roosevelt, stated, "C.F. Murphy and his kind must, like the noxious weed, be plucked out." Ever the ambitious politician, Roosevelt would soon change his mind. When Murphy died, Roosevelt had this to say: "In Mr. Murphy's death, the New York City Democratic organization has lost probably the strongest and wisest leader it has had in generations ... He was a genius who kept harmony and at the same time recognized that the world moved on. It is well to remember that he helped accomplish much in the way of progressive legislation and social welfare in our state."

Murphy married late and had no children, although he did have a stepdaughter whom he treated as his own. From when he made Flynn the Bronx leader until his unexpected death two years later, they had something of a father-son relationship. There were countless weekends at Murphy's vacation house on

eastern Long Island, too many for a young man wanting to
spend time with his friends. At these weekend retreats, the
butler was always instructed to serve "the young man," that is
Flynn, coffee while the other guests were permitted whisky
(Prohibition notwithstanding). Murphy made sure Flynn got
to fill important patronage positions, which solidified his
position in the Bronx. Murphy also invited Flynn to participate
in meetings where important decisions were made.

Throughout the rest of his life Flynn would express
gratitude for the education and support he received from—as
he always called him—Mr. Murphy. Here are some of Flynn's
comments:

- "In my opinion, Mr. Murphy was the best leader
Tammany ever had and one of the wisest political overlords
New York ever had."
- "Whatever knowledge of politics I have, I learned largely
through Mr. Murphy."
- "There probably has never been a political leader with
more political sagacity."
- and "my policy followed that of Mr. Charles F. Murphy in
his relation to the press. Basically this attitude is that a
political leader is more or less in the same position as the
manager of an opera star or actor. The manager is always in the
background, while the star gets the compliments and the
flowers. In politics, as in opera and the theater, the manager
takes the abuse and the star takes the applause. I did not want
either good publicity or bad publicity. I wanted no publicity."

There were times when Murphy acted as the understanding
but not happy parent. Flynn described how, after a night in
Albany celebrating Al Smith's inauguration as governor in
January 1923, he was called to meet with Murphy, walking

past a crowd of reporters gathered outside the Tammany leader's hotel suite. When Flynn entered the room, Murphy asked him where he had been and Flynn replied that he had spent the night "celebrating the restoration of Democratic rule in New York State." Murphy noted that Flynn "looked it," and proceeded to read a newspaper. Flynn also picked up a paper, but then fell asleep for two or three hours. When he awoke, Murphy, still reading, "looked up quizzically and said simply, 'go home and go to bed.' " As most people had only five- or ten-minute audiences with Murphy, the reporters, seeing Flynn leave after such a long period, were most impressed.

8 SAINT OR SINNER

We need to dwell a bit on Charles Francis Murphy. He was not only a mentor and supporter of Flynn, but also crucial to the careers of Al Smith and Robert Wagner, the United States senator most responsible for the passage of the New Deal legislation. History has been kind to Murphy in that he is seen as an honest, competent and public-spirited boss, and an argument in favor of the political machine. But does Murphy deserve his good reputation? The answer goes to the heart of the machine model.

As already noted, Murphy succeeded the corrupt Richard Croker as the Tammany boss in 1902. Reformers didn't expect much improvement. One of eight children of Irish Catholic immigrants, Murphy grew up in the "gas house district" near the large gas tanks on the lower East Side. His father died young—so common among immigrant families—and Murphy left school at age 14 to support his mother and siblings. One of his early jobs was as a horse-car driver on a cross-town line.

At age 24, Murphy opened the first of what would be a chain of four saloons, offering a stein of beer and a bowl of soup for five cents. No women or profanity allowed, and Murphy himself, to quote historian Matthew Lifflander, "did not smoke, swear or gamble, drank only rarely and made it very clear that he did not tolerate off-color jokes."

For ten years before becoming the Tammany boss, Murphy had been the Democratic district leader for the old gas-house area, holding office every evening on the corner of Twentieth Street and Second Avenue opposite one of his saloons. Known as "the silent boss," he would listen to his constituents seeking employment or other things, and he would deliver the needed help in a direct and open way. As Lifflander pointed out, "Murphy's personal brand of political leadership was distinguished by a determined effort to help his district morally stray less. Trusting his own moral compass, he opposed any form of graft in connection with saloons, gambling or prostitution at a time when such corruption and police payoffs were rampant throughout the city of New York."

Here is Flynn on Murphy, reflecting a view that Roosevelt, Smith and Wagner also embraced: "One thing that I learned from ... Charles F. Murphy of Tammany Hall was a firm belief in the strength of clean government. Mr. Murphy did not believe that politics should have anything to do with either gambling or prostitution. He further believed that politicians should have very little or nothing to do with the Police Department or the school system. He also believed in efficient public officers ... Mr. Murphy had no hesitation in firing a person who was dishonest or lazy. He always said that there were plenty of men in the organization who were both honest and capable and who could fill any job. The thought has always stuck with me, and I have inevitably followed Mr. Murphy's rule in making appointments or nominations."

And yet, as all those close to him knew, Murphy had grown rich through government connections, not his saloons or non-existent Tammany salary. Aside from his townhouse on East 18th Street, with what Flynn described as an "overly elegant" parlor, Murphy had a 50-acre estate in what is now called Hampton Bays on eastern Long Island, complete with a nine-hole golf course. Periodically the reform press would raise questions about Murphy's financial interests—there were cartoons in which he appeared in stripes—but no charges were ever brought against him. Warren Moscow, the longtime political reporter for *The New York Times*, noted: "When Murphy died he left an estate valued at $2 million, even though he had no visible means of support during the period of his political leadership...." Two million in 1924 would be $28 million today.

A century may have passed, but it is not hard to see how Murphy acquired his wealth. While he was still a district leader, his predecessor as Tammany boss, the infamous Mr. Croker, arranged for Mayor Robert Van Wyck (now remembered by the highway named after him, fittingly universally mispronounced as he was nothing but a Tammany front man) to appoint Murphy one of four city dock commissioners. The commissioners chose who would have access to the city's docks. During the four years he served as a commissioner, Murphy somehow acquired a great many shares of the American Ice Company, which had an ice delivery monopoly on the city docks. Even more interesting, during Murphy's last year as a commissioner, 1901, he helped found a family company—his ownership share was never disclosed—which leased two piers from the city at an annual rent of $4800 and then immediately re-leased the property for $65,000.

The company, The New York Construction and Trucking Company, went on to do a great deal of work for the city and for companies with city contracts and franchises. For example, once the Pennsylvania Rail Road agreed to employ New York Construction to do excavations necessary to build Penn Station, the railroad received the city's long-delayed permission to begin construction.

So Murphy wasn't such a saint, unless one wishes to distinguish between honest and dishonest graft. It is time to reintroduce George Washington Plunkett, who, while a public servant, made a fortune in construction and real estate. He had no trouble making a distinction "between honest graft and graft. There's all the difference in the world between the two. Yes, many of our men have grown rich in politics. I have myself. I've made a big fortune out of the game, and I'm gettin' richer every day, but I've not gone in for dishonest graft—blackmailin', gamblers, saloonkeepers, disorderly people, etc.—and neither have any of the men who have made big fortunes in politics. There's an honest graft and I'm an example of how it works. I might sum up the whole thing by saying, 'I seen my opportunities and I took 'em.'"

Tammany and the other urban machines had a more positive view of public welfare than did many of the reform anti-machine groups. Welfare was for those who needed it, not just those who deserved it. As long-time Tammany stalwart Tim Sullivan put it, "I never ask a hungry man about his past. I feed him not because he is good, but because he needs food." The only glaring exception to this generous spirit was when it came to African-Americans, who were seen as rivals at the lowest levels of the employment chain.

Over his 22 years as Tammany chairman, Murphy became increasingly supportive of government action to help the disadvantaged. This was particularly true after the Triangle Shirtwaist Factory fire of 1911, when 146 mostly young women were caught in the building and died. Two Murphy men mentioned earlier—Wagner, then the state senate majority leader, and Smith, the state assembly leader—led the largely successful effort to pass worker reform and safety laws.

As Flynn noted years later, Murphy supported Wagner and Smith because it was both the right thing to do and good politics. Flynn described Murphy as having "a real belief that government might, through an expansion of its functions, serve the people in new and helpful ways. But he was also interested in having the Democratic Party become the instrument through which those necessary reforms might come about."

There was something else that motivated Murphy: the possibility that his man Smith might become the first Catholic president. According to Flynn, "I am sure that he [Murphy] looked beyond the Governorship to Smith's future availability for the Presidency ... He wanted to be the means through which one of 'his boys' should attain the highest office in the land."

Although Governor Smith followed Murphy's patronage recommendations, it was also understood between them that the governor made the final decision on people and policy. When Smith became governor the first time, 1919, Murphy said to him, "I shall be asking you for things ... If I ever ask you to do anything which you think would impair your record as a great governor, just tell me so and that will be the end of it."

This willingness of the powerful boss to give the elected official wide latitude is something Flynn saw firsthand. He later remembered, "I was with Mr. Murphy many times when he was in Albany and so I had an opportunity to hear him discuss major appointments with the Governor. Invariably Mr. Murphy would accede to the wishes of Governor Smith."

There was at least one time, however, when Murphy pushed Smith further than the governor wanted to go. Prohibition became the law of the land in 1920, and remained a hot issue nationally and within the Democratic Party until its repeal more than a decade later. The large southern wing of the party was "dry" (pro-Prohibition) while the urban northern wing was "wet" (against Prohibition). New York State had a "baby Volstead Act" supplementing federal enforcement of Prohibition, and Murphy wanted it repealed. The legislature agreed, but Governor Smith, while no advocate of Prohibition, worried that his presidential chances would be hurt by his signing the repeal.

A discussion was in order. A meeting was arranged one weekend at an inn in eastern Long Island, and Murphy insisted that Flynn attend. Flynn described the meeting: "Quietly but firmly he [Murphy] told Smith, 'Al, you will either sign the bill (repealing the pro-Prohibition law) or I will never support you again, either for the presidency or for the governorship.' Whereupon he got up and left the room ... Smith signed the bill." Flynn believed Murphy rightly saw this signing as furthering Smith's interests, even if Smith didn't. Murphy went on to organize the campaign for Smith to receive the 1924 Democratic presidential nomination.

Murphy would not live to see his dreams for Smith realized—in fact, no one would. On April 25, 1924, just as Al Smith's campaign for the Democratic presidential nomination was gathering steam, Murphy dropped dead of a heart attack. Had Murphy lived, would Smith have been nominated in 1924, as he was four years later? Flynn thought not and believed that, had Murphy lived, he would have seen that Smith couldn't make it in 1924, and convinced Smith to concede early and not let the voting go to 103 ballots. With Murphy's death, Smith came to assume, to quote Flynn, "active direction of his own candidacy. I believe it to be axiomatic that the opinion of a man who is a candidate for public office is not dependable in matters of political organization ... He [Smith] was unable to grasp the extent of the wholly illogical but powerful opposition to him as a New Yorker, a Tammany man, a 'wet', and Roman Catholic." Flynn found one exception to his rule that candidates should not run their own campaigns: Franklin Roosevelt.

9 BOSS OF THE BRONX

So it came to pass—to take up where we left off two chapters ago—that Ed Flynn, just 30 years old and never having served as a district leader, became the Democratic boss of the Bronx, a title he used happily for the rest of his life. By simply assuming office he found himself in the middle of a bitter intra-party fight. The party was ready to nominate Al Smith as its candidate for governor in 1922, Smith having won in 1918 and lost in the Republican landslide of 1920. However, William Randolph Hearst, the powerful newspaper publisher, wanted the U.S. senate nomination, and Smith made it clear that he would not run on the same ticket with Hearst. The two men were bitter rivals.

At the state party's convention in September, things came to a head. Brooklyn's population had by now surpassed Manhattan's and the Brooklyn party boss, John McCooey, supported Hearst. So did Mayor John Hylan, loyal member of the Brooklyn machine. Murphy, seemingly uncommitted on the Hearst nomination but actually opposed, invited various delegate leaders to discuss the situation with him, and Flynn was flattered to be included in the meetings. Murphy succeeded in achieving his desired result, and Hearst withdrew before any vote was taken.

Flynn was even more flattered when Murphy, in control of the convention, told him he could choose the candidate for secretary of state, then an elective office. This was the first time the Bronx had ever been given the opportunity to select a statewide candidate, and Flynn chose a distinguished doctor who had once been his teacher in public school. The entire Democratic ticket was elected in November, and Flynn's ability to bring home some bacon to the Bronx was, in his words, "a definite indication that Mr. Murphy stood firmly behind me. It is probable that this nomination did more than anything else to consolidate my position in the Bronx organization."

Upon succeeding in regaining the governorship, Smith, with Murphy's strong support until his death shortly before the national convention, made a run for the 1924 Democratic presidential nomination. Flynn, who considered Smith a genuine friend as well as close political colleague, was totally on board, but always felt, as previously noted, that the party wasn't ready to nominate Smith. In the election, the Democratic nominee, John W. Davis, was badly defeated by Calvin Coolidge but Smith was re-elected governor.

While in most places the political class can relax a bit after a presidential election, no such luxury awaits the New York City crowd. Mayoral elections, always the year after presidential contests, hold the keys to local patronage and thus the well-being of party organizations. In 1925, Mayor Hylan wanted a third term, and he had in support our old friends McCooey (Brooklyn) and Hearst (see Orson Wells' *Citizen Kane*). McCooey saw himself as the late Charles Murphy's successor as the city's most powerful party boss, and his counterparts in Queens and Staten Island were also in Hylan's camp.

Governor Smith was not for Hylan. The Hearst connection may have been part of it, but he also shared with Flynn a belief, as Flynn put it, that Hylan "had shown himself to be a fundamentally weak Mayor, and his personal capacity was altogether too meager to meet the problems of a great and growing city." With Smith and George W. Olvaney, Tammany's compromise and reluctant successor to Murphy, on his side, Flynn took the lead in opposing Hylan.

For the young boss of the Bronx, this was a serious decision. As he later reflected, "Had I failed in my opposition to Hylan, I have no doubt but that I would have been eliminated as Leader of the Bronx. Mayor Hylan, if re-elected, would have brought all the power of the city government against me, and while I would have retained the support of Governor Smith, it is unlikely that I would have resisted the resentment on the part of many political leaders in the Bronx over my having alienated City Hall."

After considering a great many possible candidates to oppose Hylan, Flynn, with the concurrence of Smith and Olvaney, settled on James J. Walker, the Democratic leader in the state senate. Just as there was a downside risk to Flynn that Hylan might win, he recognized the upside of a Walker victory. As he wrote, "I was not unaware of the added prestige I would attain should Walker be nominated. Tammany Hall would be under heavy obligation to me because of the support I offered at a crucial time. The Bronx was growing, and New York County [Manhattan] was losing population. Ultimately, it seemed to me, the Bronx would be the senior partner in this coalition of the western counties."

About Walker, Flynn noted, "His quickness and a great personal charm combined to overcome opposition far more often than was justified by the merits of the points at issue. No one in New York politics was more personable or more generally liked than Jimmy Walker. No one could ever become really angry with him." While Walker—"Beau James"— would leave office in disgrace, having surrounded himself with charlatans and outright crooks, Flynn believed "that he was never personally dishonest."

Walker won both the primary and election, and, as one of his first official acts, appointed Flynn chamberlain of the city. Having resigned as sheriff at the end of 1925, Flynn would serve as chamberlain from 1926 until 1928. Although the new job came with a good salary ($12,000 a year, compared with the $10,000 as sheriff), there wasn't much to it other than acting as a custodian of public funds. Flynn, as he had with the sheriff's office, came to think that the chamberlain's office should be eliminated, as it later was. He mused, "I certainly can derive no personal prestige from the fact that I have held two offices that came to be recognized as expendable, that of the Sheriff of the Bronx, and that of City Chamberlain of New York."

While serving as chamberlain, Flynn also formed a law partnership with Monroe Goldwater, a fellow delegate from the Bronx at the 1924 Democratic convention for whom he had clerked while in law school. Flynn's children remember Goldwater, a distinguished trial lawyer and prominent member of the Jewish philanthropic community, as their father's closest friend. Mrs. Goldwater was their mother's best friend. The firm, Goldwater and Flynn, with what one commentator described as "luxurious" offices in the Lincoln Building on 42nd Street near Grand Central Station, was a success. To quote historian Jill Jannos, it was "the prominent political law firm in New York City." It was considered entirely acceptable for Flynn to maintain a private practice while remaining Bronx Democratic leader and serving as chamberlain and later secretary of state of New York, just as many state legislators still maintain private practices.

What does a law firm with political connections offer a client? The obvious answer is access to the right people. Goldwater and Flynn benefited from Flynn's connections, and he would not have seen anything wrong with this. He once wrote, "There are many businessmen who while their businesses have no actual connection with either government or politics, feel that having a friend at court in a political position may at some time be of benefit to them. This does not mean that they have to obtain illegal favors. Many things can be done for them that are not wrong." Years after Ed Flynn's death, Charles Dolan of the CATV cable franchise, would retain Ed's son Richard, formerly a partner at Goldwater and Flynn, because "Dick is politically able, and we are obtaining these permissions from a political body."

Goldwater and Flynn was unique in one regard: when the firm was retained for its political access, it also insisted on performing the related legal work. According to Warren Moscow, "Political law firms were accustomed to accepting fees for allowing their names to appear on briefs while other firms did the work. The lawyer with an 'in' might get $10,000, and those who did the work, $40,000. Goldwater and Flynn combined the operation, insisting on using their skill as well as their 'in' to collect the entire $50,000." According to Robert Caro, "During the decades in which Flynn made the power, Goldwater made the money—millions, perhaps tens of millions—for both of them." Sometimes potential business was turned away as being too political: for example, seeking a zoning change to allow for the construction of a gas station in the Bronx.

Flynn certainly wasn't the only lawyer to attract clients because of his political connections. His successor, in a sense, at the city and state levels was Bill Shea, product of the Brooklyn Democratic organization, of whom it was said that he had no idea where the courthouses were located. His firm, Shea Gould, was known as "Blarney and Chutzpah." In a 1974 profile in *The New Yorker*, Nicholas Pileggi described Shea as Flynn might have been described a generation earlier, "the unofficial chairman of the state's permanent government." He brought National League baseball back to New York and the Mets' former Shea Stadium was named in his honor. On the national level, Clark Clifford, the man most behind Truman's victory in 1948, was also the man to see to move things through several administrations.

10 MANNING THE STORE

While Murphy was his mentor and model, Flynn also did things his own way. As Richard Rovere noted in a 1945 profile in *The New Yorker*, Flynn operated with "a fundamental disregard for the entire theory and practice of bossism." Rovere observed that it was standard operating practice for the party boss to display "the common touch. This means ... that he can rule so long as he lives like a democrat ... he must not let his standard of living rise visibly above the people around him ... accessibility is another undisputed requirement. A boss must always be available to his subordinates in the machine from whose ranks he has presumably risen, and the most successful bosses are like Machiavelli's good prince, as attractive to the plaza as they are to the palace."

Flynn would have nothing of this conventional wisdom. Rovere estimated that Flynn divided his time about equally among politics, his law practice and real estate holdings, and personal pursuits. He saw his assembly district leaders on a strict and limited schedule. "He would never think of attending a clambake or passing out Christmas baskets to poor though registered citizens, and the party workers and voters on whom his power rests all know that he is one of the most difficult men in the city to find, let alone to see." Rovere did note that Flynn on occasion suffered from two "Irish weaknesses," melancholy and drink. He was also known for constantly smoking and chewing gum. Flynn's children disagree that their father was particularly melancholy and believe his drinking never went beyond normal social practices.

As for raising operating funds for the county party, most political machines, including Tammany, assessed patronage job holders a percentage of their salaries, usually at least five percent. Those holding elective positions were required to contribute flat sums. In the Bronx under Flynn, however, the required jobholder contribution was, to quote the boss himself, "a very loosely enforced rule ... many office holders do not contribute, and for a variety of reasons. There may be a sickness in the family. Or there may be any number of reasons, which they can satisfactorily explain, to secure exemption from contributing. The individual never suffers if his explanation is truthful and sincere."

Flynn's standard of living reflected his considerable wealth, and he made no attempt to hide either. His penthouse apartment along the Hudson River in the Riverdale section of the Bronx—sometimes called "Ed's gothic aerie"—included 13 rooms and several porches and solariums. It had its own entrance and elevator. In time, there was a country place, a horse farm in Maryland and part ownership in a 50,000-acre ranch in Nevada, later bought by Bing Crosby. Rovere wrote, "Flynn keeps his home as a preserve for Mrs. Flynn, their three children and his close friends." His extensive library included biographies, English literature and history. The Flynns also collected etchings by Joseph Pennell. In an October 1940 issue of *The Saturday Evening Post*, an article by former White House aide Raymond Moley titled "Boss Flynn Can't Lose" caught an important Flynn quality, "He had broad interests of which politics was but one." Flynn would have a good life regardless of the election outcome.

The October 1942 *Time* cover story on Flynn reported, "But the Bronx apartment, where the big freckled Boss likes to sit playing Russian band and gin rummy with his attractive, apolitical wife, is Flynn's pride and joy. The home is home: Flynn has tried to keep his home life a thing apart. He chews gum, smokes a lot, wears Charvet ties of extraordinary loudness, and sincerely believes he has never taken a political job, but has always been shoved into each one."

The years between the world wars were still a time when the Protestant establishment kept its distance from, among others, the rising Irish Catholics. Joe Kennedy chose Hyannis Port for his summer home after being socially rejected elsewhere. Joseph M. Bailey, the legionary Democratic boss of Connecticut who was so important to Jack Kennedy's rise to the presidency, was refused membership in a country club near Hartford because—at least as he saw it—he was Irish Catholic. Of course, being a Democrat might not have helped. Flynn, perhaps because he lived more in the orbit of New York than Boston, does not seem to have faced such overt discrimination. He joined the Mahopac Country Club near his country place, although his children remember him commenting that he may have been the club's first Catholic member.

At the club, Flynn occasionally played golf, but not regularly or seriously. Sports were not his thing, and he used to joke that his friends who had kept up with their sports all died young. He did ride as a young man, but not after he had a bad fall from a horse. While his children have no memory of his riding, his oldest son has a photograph of Flynn and Roosevelt astride horses, with the president wearing long dark pants covering his crippled legs. What was F.D.R. doing on a horse? Flynn's children believe that the photograph may have been taken for political purposes during the 1932 presidential campaign to show Roosevelt as less disabled than he actually was.

The Flynn children—in order, Patrick, Richard and Sheila—remember their childhood with great fondness. Their father would hold forth at the dining table in Riverdale, often with their boarding school or college friends as guests. Conversation was lively and humorous, with their father perfectly willing to be provocative. While the children had a privileged upbringing, their parents actively discouraged social pretense. When Patrick graduated from Canterbury School, he listed Riverdale as his address. His father mentioned to him that the family was really from the Bronx. The children remember their father's closest friends as a varied lot: Monroe Goldwater; Averell Harriman of the railroad fortune; Earle Brown, the African-American *Life* photographer; "Sell 'em" Ben Smith and Michael Meehan of the wild Wall Street 1920s; Herbert Lehman; several men with whom he grew up in the old neighborhood; and the Roosevelts. They also remember Flynn speaking out strongly against any kind of ethnic, racial or religious discrimination.

In one important regard, Flynn was an absolutely conventional political boss. He understood that, for him to stay in power and have patronage to offer, candidates he supported had to win. Flynn's children describe him as "coldly pragmatic," "tough minded," "realistic" and "always logical" when it came to politics. Here is Flynn on candidate selections: "A political leader, as a 'Boss,' must not only be able to pick his man, but he must be able to 'guess right.' During my leadership I have been lucky enough to do this in many political situations." He went on to mention his, and the Bronx Democratic Party's, support of Walker over Mayor Hylan, Roosevelt over Smith in 1932, and Governor Lehman as FDR's successor in Albany. Flynn concluded, "All these things together have helped to build my strength as a leader. My [assembly district] leaders realize that I have usually guessed right. It has put the Bronx organization in the forefront in various campaigns ...."

11 TWO AMBITIOUS MEN

Helen and Ed Flynn married in 1927. A graduate of Morris High School in the Bronx, Helen then had taken business courses and become one of the first tax examiners at the I.R.S. Her sister married the labor leader George Meany, later head of the A.F.L-C.I.O., the country's giant union federation. A first child died shortly after birth, and then came two boys and a girl. Secure in his position as Bronx Democratic leader, Flynn hoped to spend much of his time developing his law practice with Monroe Goldwater. He had no personal political ambition beyond what he had already achieved. Politics kept intruding, however, as did his personal and political relationships with two able and ambitious men, Alfred E. Smith and Franklin D. Roosevelt.

Al Smith came up the hard way. In order to support his family after his father's death, he left school at 14 and worked for seven years at the Fulton Fish Market. Under the tutelage of Charles Murphy, and with such colleagues as Robert Wagner and Frances Perkins, Smith rose through the ranks to be elected governor of New York in 1918. Defeated in the Republican landslide of 1920, he was re-elected in 1922, 1924, and 1926 to what were then two-year terms. As already noted, he—both as a state assembly leader and governor—supported legislation to insure fire and worker safety, limit working hours for women and children, and in other ways directly involve the government in public welfare. He was a "wet," an opponent of the 1924 federal restrictions on immigration and a supporter of top aide Robert Moses's expansion of the state parks system. What Smith achieved in New York in the 1920s Roosevelt (and other New Yorkers including Wagner in the senate, and Perkins as secretary of labor) would take to the federal level a decade later. As one commentator put it, "Before the Roosevelt revolution there was the Smith revolution."

It is clear that Flynn, 18 years younger, adored Smith. He described their friendship as "intimate." He believed in Smith's legislative achievements, and found him honest, effective and very funny. During the 1928 presidential campaign, Smith, the first Catholic major party candidate, was traveling by train through anti-Catholic territory in the southwest. It was late at night, and as Smith looked out the window he saw burning crosses protesting his candidacy. He turned to his closest aide, Joseph Proskauer, a prominent New York lawyer and Jewish leader, and exclaimed, "Joe, they must have known you were aboard."

During Smith's governorship Flynn served as a political advisor and patronage dispenser. He was also useful in raising campaign funds. He introduced Smith to John J. Raskob, a prominent businessman whom Smith arranged to become chairman of the Democratic national committee. Of course, sometimes Flynn's efforts on behalf of Smith were more prosaic. As he later recalled, "The Governor's mansion in Albany, during the Smith regime, was never really arid. A cocktail or highball, in fact, was always available." Once, when Flynn was meeting with Smith and others in the mansion, Josephus Daniels, a prominent North Carolina Democrat and secretary of the navy during World War I, was announced. He was a strong supporter of Prohibition. According to Flynn, Smith sent him to meet with Daniels, while the others hid the "many cocktail shakers, bottles of liquor, and glasses ... those evidences of conviviality." The governor then met with Daniels in "a most conventional and dispirited atmosphere."

Roosevelt and Flynn served as Smith delegates at the 1924 convention. Close as he was to Smith, Flynn would grow even closer to Roosevelt, finally sacrificing his friendship with Smith by giving vital support to Roosevelt in the 1932 nomination battle. Flynn described his relationship with Roosevelt as being "very deep and affectionate," but he also recognized that "because our relationship was so close and our principal interests were political, it was almost impossible to separate personal affairs from political."

Franklin Roosevelt, nine years Flynn's senior and born to great privilege, was elected as a Democrat—his father's party—to the state senate from Dutchess County in 1910. He resigned from the senate when President Woodrow Wilson appointed him assistant secretary of the navy in 1913. In the senate, he was an outspoken opponent of his party's urban machines best represented by Tammany Hall, a position required of anyone representing upstate rural communities. In 1920, despite his youth and modest experience, he was the Democratic Party's vice presidential candidate, evidence of the importance of New York and the Roosevelt name. The Republican ticket of Harding and Coolidge, promising a return to "normalcy" after World War I, defeated the Democratic ticket in a landslide.

One historian has called the Democratic Party of the early 20th century the party of "vacillating conservatism." Things were changing, however. The urban, Catholic and union wings of the party were increasingly powerful at the expense of the old guard of white southerners, "dries," populists and western farmers. Smith's failure to receive the nomination in 1924 and his success in 1928 reflected the party's changing composition.

Young Franklin Roosevelt, whose presidential ambition had begun in childhood, saw what was happening and made his peace with the party bosses. While serving as assistant secretary of the navy in 1917, he agreed to speak at the Tammany Hall Independence Day rally as a guest of Charles Murphy. FDR began his talk, odd as it may sound, "If Tammany could stand to have him, he would stand to come."

Roosevelt contracted polio in 1921, and remained severely disabled for the rest of his life. He and his devoted aide Louis Howe corresponded with party leaders across the nation, many of whom Roosevelt had met during the 1920 campaign. He nominated Smith—"the happy warrior"—for president at both the 1924 and the 1928 conventions. Beginning in 1926, he began speaking out on the obligation for government to deal directly with social and economic needs.

12 1928

Culturally and politically, Al Smith and Ed Flynn were on the same team, which was to the benefit of both men. Flynn noted, "Al Smith, during his time as governor, was a shining symbol and proof of the theory that one can serve the people and his party at the same time." As for their personal relationship, Flynn remembered years later, "As time went on my acquaintance with Governor Smith ripened into a genuine friendship. I was often invited to the Governor's Mansion and, needless to say I always accepted."

While the Democratic convention, after 103 ballots in the heat of a New York summer, failed to select Smith in 1924, it did nominate him on the first ballot four years later. Immediately upon his nomination and concerned with carrying New York, Smith asked Flynn, whom he knew to be close to Roosevelt, to convince FDR to run for governor. Smith believed Roosevelt "would add the greatest strength to the ticket" of any possible gubernatorial candidate.

There followed a series of phone calls from Flynn to Roosevelt, who was at the rehabilitation center in Warm Springs, Georgia, which he founded after he had contracted polio. As there was only one phone at the facility, communications were difficult. They were made more so by the fact that Roosevelt did not want to run. He, and Louis Howe, thought 1928 was too early for him to re-enter the political arena, both men long focused on the presidency and assuming that the White House would not be available until the completion of Hoover's second term in 1936. Also, the Warm Springs center had some serious financial issues that Roosevelt had to address.

Flynn succeeded, after many calls to both Roosevelt and Smith, and after John Raskob agreed to help on the Warm Springs financial situation. Flynn believed that Roosevelt, in agreeing to run, had made a great personal sacrifice in that "he was foreclosing the hope that he could make further marked improvements in his physical condition." Herbert Lehman of the prominent Jewish banking family accepted the nomination for lieutenant governor, which was particularly fortunate as the Republican candidate for governor, Albert Ottinger, was Jewish.

Smith was right that Roosevelt would strengthen the ticket. In truth, they both needed each other. The Smith connection offered Roosevelt acceptance by the party's machines, while Roosevelt gave Smith the cover of old Protestant America. As Smith supporter Joseph Proskauer told him, "You're a Bowery mick and he is a Protestant patrician and he'd take some of the curse off you."

There is a long tradition of political machines nominating prominent and seemingly independent people for positions at or near the top of the ticket as a way of increasing the entire ticket's appeal. Longtime aficionados of New York politics are fond of the story about Hymie Schorenstein, a Democratic district leader who served as Brooklyn's registrar of deeds although he could neither read nor write. When a down-ballot candidate asked Schorenstein why the party spent so much of its money in support of Roosevelt at the top of the ticket, he replied, "Ah, you're worried? Listen. Did you ever go down to the wharf to see the Staten Island Ferry come in? You ever watch it, and look down in the water at all those chewing-gum wrappers, and the banana peels and all the garbage? When the ferryboat comes into the wharf, automatically it pulls all the garbage in, too. The name of the ferryboat is Franklin D. Roosevelt—stop worrying!"

Governor Smith asked Flynn to oversee the Smith and Roosevelt campaigns in New York. As soon as Roosevelt returned to New York, he met with Smith and Flynn. They agreed that Louis Howe, the Albany reporter who had been Roosevelt's closest political aide since 1911, should manage the gubernatorial campaign. Flynn would later say of Howe, "His loyalty to Roosevelt was a beautiful thing. I am sure that he would willingly have given up his life to advance Roosevelt's political fortunes."

Howe was protective of Roosevelt, and discouraged him from getting personally close to others out of fear that they might have hidden agendas. This was not the case, however, with Flynn, in whom he had great trust. Flynn later reflected, "Louis Howe was extremely jealous and suspicious of anyone who appeared to become too friendly with Roosevelt. I think it is only fair to say that Howe felt that in order to protect Roosevelt he had to be careful to supervise whatever relations Roosevelt had with other people. However I had been one of the few people who got along with Howe. I had always been careful to make things clear between us ... I had no political ambitions or ax to grind."

During the 1928 campaign, there was one issue about which Roosevelt, to his great credit, went further than Howe thought wise. According to Flynn, "There is no question but that Roosevelt emphasized the Smith candidacy at the expense of his own in upstate New York. Day after day he preached tolerance in opposition to the serious growth of anti-Catholicism that was abroad in the land. In fact Roosevelt's emphasis on Smith's candidacy disturbed Louis Howe so much that he warned Roosevelt to remember that he was also a candidate and ought to look more closely to his own interests. This advice Roosevelt ignored."

Nineteen twenty-eight was a good year for Republicans, although things would begin to change dramatically a year later. On election night, Roosevelt, Howe, Flynn and other party leaders gathered at the Roosevelt Hotel. It became evident early that Herbert Hoover had beaten Smith badly, even carrying five southern states. The Electoral College vote was 444 to 87. Maybe more surprisingly, Smith had failed to carry New York. Almost everyone assumed that Roosevelt had lost the governor's race as well.

In fact, Roosevelt won. As Flynn painted the scene, "About midnight Roosevelt went home. Louis Howe also departed for parts unknown; I was left with one or two others. I began to analyze the upstate returns, which were coming in with their usual slowness. They showed that Roosevelt was running quite considerably ahead of Governor Smith. I started to figure what might be the outcome of this situation. At about one o'clock in the morning or perhaps later, I concluded from my study of these returns that Roosevelt was actually elected. But to convince anyone else of that was difficult. In fact, when I called Roosevelt on the telephone and told him it was my opinion that he had been elected, he said that I was wrong and crazy to wake him up."

By 2 a.m., with the early editions of the New York papers announcing Roosevelt's defeat, Flynn became worried that the upstate returns were being withheld in order to make possible the later reporting of false results. He decided to take action, proceeding to inform the press that a hundred Democratic lawyers were on their way upstate to guard against election fraud in a thousand or so rural districts yet to report results.

In fact, to quote Richard Rovere, "There was no band of crusading lawyers; even if there had been, they probably could have done nothing. But the announcement brought in the returns from most of the laggard districts in a few hours."

It was a complete bluff, but it worked. By morning it was clear Roosevelt had won by a little more than 25,000 votes. When Flynn—having been up 36 hours—arrived at Roosevelt's house with the good news, the governor-elect was still in bed.

13 ROOSEVELT THE GOVERNOR

Although Flynn spent his entire adult life deeply involved with politics, there were times when he seemed happy to walk away from it all. One such time was immediately after Roosevelt's gubernatorial victory in 1928. The Flynns had just lost their first child at birth. As Flynn himself put it, "Since my political duties had taken me away from my home so consistently over the years, I now felt an obligation to my wife to eliminate needless intrusions into our private lives and any extraneous demands on my time." As would always happen, Flynn couldn't stay away for very long.

Soon after the election, the Flynns embarked on what was to be a six-month trip to Europe, with Ed having made clear that he planned to step down as the Bronx party boss when he returned. Roosevelt would have none of it. He wanted Flynn to join his administration as secretary of state, a position with light duties that would allow Ed to continue his law practice, head the Bronx party, and act as a top political advisor and patronage dispenser. As the Flynns traveled to London, Paris and Rome, Roosevelt's transatlantic telephone calls and cables followed. Flynn's answer was always no.

Finally, a cable from Roosevelt arrived in Rome that, in Flynn's words, "implored me, if I would not reconsider the offer [of secretary of state], at least to come back to New York City to talk over the entire situation. I realized that a good deal more than my personal problem of whether or not to accept the office was involved. The future relations of Roosevelt and Smith were concerned, and, since I was deeply in the confidence of both men, I felt it my duty to return." This would not be the only instance when Flynn found himself caught between these two powerful men.

Arriving home on Christmas Eve, Flynn went directly from the ship to the governor-elect's house on 65th Street. Roosevelt turned on the charm: "Eddie, when you were insisting that I run for Governor, you said that I owed a duty to the party to accept. I am now saying to you that you owe a similar duty to the party to accept the office [of secretary of state]." For what would not be the last time, Flynn surrendered to Roosevelt's pleadings and accepted a job he really didn't want.

The formal duties of the secretary of state were few—mostly the regulation of a number of professions (real estate brokers and notaries public, for example) and businesses (cemeteries, professional sports). Raymond Moley, in his previously mentioned article, estimated that Flynn spent only a day a week at the job. The real value of the position to a governor was that it offered a perch for a political advisor and a fix-it man, a role Robert Moses, New York's famous parks and highway builder, played as Smith's secretary of state. Flynn believed that the most important reason Roosevelt wanted him to become secretary of state was that, contrary to Smith's strong advice, "Roosevelt did not want to appoint Moses."

There is a back story. Al Smith, defeated for president in 1928 and no longer governor, assumed that Roosevelt, his successor, would welcome his continued presence in Albany. In fact, Smith seemed to expect that the incoming administration would operate as a sort of regency with him in control. He even rented an apartment at the DeWitt Clinton Hotel near the Capitol. Roosevelt, however, wasn't interested in a Smith regency. As Flynn noted, "Having been elected

Governor on his own merits ... Roosevelt was determined to go it on his own. He felt that he would be better off completely divorced from Smith's influence." Flynn was the ideal candidate to replace Moses. He was a friend and supporter of Smith who also was a fellow Irish Catholic regular Democrat. Smith couldn't complain, or at least never did publicly.

It was also true that Roosevelt and Moses disliked each other. Roosevelt had served on the Taconic State Park Commission, which operated as part of the state parks system that Moses oversaw. One story is that he resented Moses for directing state highway money to his Long Island parkways that would otherwise have gone to the Hudson Valley. Another is that Moses alienated Roosevelt by refusing to appoint Louis Howe to a largely no-show parks position, knowing that Howe really would be working to further Roosevelt's political future. Perhaps there is some truth to both stories. In 1934, Moses ran unsuccessfully as the Republican candidate for governor against Herbert Lehman.

Soon after becoming governor, Roosevelt asked Flynn to represent New York on the Democratic national committee. This was Flynn's first political foray outside the state, and he continued as national committeeman, with all its important contacts, until his death 23 years later. Within New York, Flynn oversaw the dispensing of patronage, and both he and Roosevelt recognized the need to build the party upstate. Roosevelt made a point of traveling everywhere, and getting to know the local party people. The patronage jobs were reserved for party loyalists. To quote Flynn, "My estimate is that ninety percent of the men and women appointed by the Governor to jobs in the state were enrolled Democrats and workers of the various Democratic organizations."

Was this party building just for the sake of winning elections, or were there public policy purposes as well? For

Roosevelt and Flynn, policy and politics went together. Roosevelt once told his White House aide Samuel Rosenman, "You have to get the votes first—then you can do the good works." According to Rosenman, "Roosevelt taught me how closely those two subjects were intertwined."

The stock market crash of October 1929 heralded the beginning of the Depression. Roosevelt recognized, in his words, "There is a duty on the part of government to do something about this." Continuing many of Smith's policy initiatives, Roosevelt supported increased unemployment insurance, labor reforms, more public works, public utility expansion, lower taxes for farmers and other initiatives he would later bring to Washington with the New Deal.

New York Democrats went on the offensive to re-elect Roosevelt governor in 1930. The party produced "talking movies" containing speeches by Roosevelt, Smith, Wagner and others that were a big hit upstate. It also created a naturalized citizen bureau with 28 divisions, one for each national group, with literature in Yiddish, Italian and several other languages. Roosevelt was re-elected with 62 percent of the vote and a plurality of 725,000. He carried New York City and 41 of the state's 57 counties outside the city. The coattails were short, however, as the Democrats did not take control of the state senate until 1932, and the assembly until 1934.

In late November 1930, not long after his reelection, Roosevelt asked Flynn to spend the night at the governor's mansion. After dinner, Roosevelt, Flynn and Howe retired to the library, where Roosevelt voiced his belief that he could become the Democratic presidential nominee in 1932. Flynn pledged his support for such an effort.

First came the need for campaign money. Flynn organized a Friends of Roosevelt group—each member donated at least $2000—to support the candidacy. Contributors included

Joseph P. Kennedy, Herbert Lehman and Roosevelt's mother Sara. Flynn recalled, "Many times during the pre-convention campaign this committee was completely out of funds, and I personally was called upon to pay the salaries of employees to keep the organization going."

Roosevelt also asked Flynn to travel the country lining up future delegates, but Flynn knew he would be miscast in such a role: "I realized my own limitations. I was not an 'easy mixer;' indeed I found it quite difficult to move about with facility among strange people ... I told Roosevelt that I preferred to remain in the background, doing such work as I knew I would do well."

If not Flynn, who? Roosevelt and Flynn agreed on someone out of central casting for the assignment, James Aloysius Farley, who had been a player in local Democratic politics for years. Farley's father having died when he was ten, his mother provided for her family by operating a grocery store and bar in Stony Point, a Hudson River town north of New York City. After high school, Farley—while in and out of the building supply business—gravitated to politics. He served as town clerk, town supervisor and state assemblyman for one term. He also held various party positions, including town Democratic chairman before he was old enough to vote. He helped manage Smith's and Roosevelt's gubernatorial campaigns, and was appointed by Smith to head the state athletic commission. At the commission, he fought against the color line drawn by white boxers not wanting to risk losing to black opponents.

A product of the party machine, Farley was also its advocate. "I am a firm believer in party politics," he wrote. "The steady climb up through party ranks is still the best training ground for American officials under our democratic system of government ... The great contribution of the political party is that ... it has allowed the United States to avoid the destructive blight of government by minority ... If party government ... should crumble ... then the United States will be at the mercy of every organized minority, every ambitious demagogue, every radio spellbinder, every crackpot who comes along."

At a time when Roosevelt's interest in the White House was confidential, Farley came with something of a cover for his outreach to party leaders across the country. He had long been active in the Benevolent and Protective Order of Elks, attending annual conventions. In the summer of 1931, he traveled to the Elks convention in Seattle, just coincidentally stopping off in 18 other places on the 19-day trip.

What Flynn, as Democratic national committeeman, and Farley, as traveling sounding board, found was a party eager for a presidential victory. In the 70 years between the Civil War and the Depression only two Democrats had made it to the White House, Grover Cleveland and Woodrow Wilson. It was looking increasingly likely that another could make it, and Roosevelt, with his resounding victory in 1930, was an obvious possibility. Farley was one of the first to go public: "I fully expect that the call will come to Governor Roosevelt ... the Democrats in the nation naturally want as their candidate for President the man who has shown himself capable of carrying the most important state in the country by a record-breaking majority."

Where was Al Smith? After his defeat in 1928, Smith stated publicly that he would never run again. In joining the Roosevelt campaign, Flynn relied on Smith's disavowal. As the Depression deepened during 1931, however, Hoover's vulnerabilities became increasingly evident and the prospects for a Democratic candidate to win in 1932 improved. The press started reporting rumors that Smith was becoming interested in another try. Flynn suggested to Roosevelt that, in order not to offend Smith unnecessarily, someone should talk to him directly about his intentions. Flynn later wrote, "The Governor turned to me and said, 'Well, if that is the case, there was no one better than you to handle this situation.' "

"This was not a particularly enjoyable task for me," Flynn later recalled. "Smith and I had been friends for many years. I admired and had genuine affection for him." However, after telling Smith that he was supporting Roosevelt for the 1932 presidential nomination, Flynn was relieved that Smith replied that "... he was completely through with politics and that no one could induce him to enter the political arena again." Herbert Lehman would have a similar conversation with Smith. The road ahead seemed clear for Roosevelt.

As noted earlier, Flynn believed candidates should not manage their own campaigns. He wrote, "A candidate's ambition gets in the way of his political judgment. He cannot view the situation objectively." Roosevelt was the exception that proved the rule: he always ran his own campaigns and did it well. In the run-up to 1932, Roosevelt had the advantage of previous experience. As the Democratic candidate for vice president in 1920, he had traveled the country—58 speeches in 53 days—and gotten to know literally hundreds of party people.

Beginning during his reelection campaign in 1930, and greatly increasing the following year, Roosevelt spoke out on national issues, advocating his state agenda as national policy. "One of the duties of the State," he said, " is that of caring for those of its citizens who find themselves the victims of such adverse circumstances as makes them unable to obtain even the necessities for mere existence without the aid of others." As historians have long noted, however, Roosevelt believed more in experimentation than in the consistent application of a political philosophy. While criticizing Hoover for not doing enough to help those in need, he also complained about Hoover's high taxes, deficit spending and policies causing the federal government to grow too large.

14 1932

Roosevelt announced his candidacy in January 1932. Al Smith, despite what he had told Flynn, Lehman and others to the contrary, followed suit the next month. The urban party machines leaned towards Smith, who easily carried the Massachusetts primary on April 1. Roosevelt was stronger in the southern, western and agricultural states. Louis Howe set up a large map of the United Sates in his office indicating the dates of the primaries and conventions. He colored the states committed to Roosevelt pink and over time this color spread. Smith joked that "lots of areas" don't necessarily mean "lots of delegates." There were several other candidates, including "favorite sons," which probably helped Roosevelt. The national Democratic Party was a mix of very different constituencies: segregationists, increasing numbers of African Americans, dries, wets, western farmers, and urban ethnics. As Will Rogers famously stated, "I am not a member of an organized political party. I am a Democrat."

Several days before the opening of the 1932 convention in Chicago, Flynn and Farley, later joined by Howe, set up headquarters in the Congress Hotel. They met with delegates, often connecting them by phone and loudspeaker with Roosevelt, who was back in New York following the longstanding practice of candidates not appearing at conventions. The Roosevelt team almost made a big mistake, which Flynn attributed to inexperience, in beginning an effort to eliminate the party rule that two-thirds of the delegates was necessary to nominate. This rule gave the south—Democratic and representing about one-third of all delegates—power it would not otherwise have. Flynn and the others soon realized they were jeopardizing Roosevelt's southern support and backed off.

The situation with the New York delegation at the convention was particularly interesting. Flynn, boss of the Bronx and national committeeman for New York, was the leader of Roosevelt forces in the state. The leaders of the other New York City counties were for Smith, while upstate leaned to Roosevelt. Flynn's strategy, as he described it, was simple: "Because Tammany was not popular with the country at large, and because in this instance the Roosevelt people were the underdogs, we decided to get as much advantage as possible in that situation. We did not hesitate to make it clear that Tammany was opposed to Roosevelt. This helped him tremendously with many of the delegates throughout the country. We tried further to bring out quietly that most of the decent Democrats in New York were supporting Roosevelt. With this in mind, we resolved in no way to contest anything that Tammany wished to do. We wanted to show the rest of the country that Tammany was riding rough-shod over the plain people of New York." As reflected in the news coverage at the time, Flynn's strategy worked.

Something else happened at the Chicago convention that Flynn would describe as "one of the saddest experiences I have ever had." Flynn had, in his words, an "intimate" relationship with Smith and his family, and was close to many of Smith's supporters, some of whom "resented" his support of Roosevelt. Urged by close Smith advisor Joseph Proskauer, Flynn decided to meet with Smith privately, and arranged to stop by his hotel suite. He wrote, "As I entered the room the people who were with him left. We were alone. He turned to me and said, 'Ed, you are not representing the people of Bronx County in your support of Roosevelt. You know the people of Bronx County want you to support me.' "

Flynn replied that Smith might be right, but that he was honor-bound to stand by his commitment to Roosevelt, a commitment made when Smith had disavowed any interest in running. As Flynn remembered, "Emotions rose," and the conversation "ended abruptly." Reflecting years later, Flynn wrote, "The simple fact was that I believed then, as I believe now, that Roosevelt was better equipped to meet the emergency of the hour than Smith, that, in any case, Smith would not have been nominated and elected."

By the opening of the convention, Flynn believed that, of the 1,154 total delegates, Roosevelt had 663, a majority but short of the required two-thirds. The entire south except Virginia was in his camp. With their majority, the Roosevelt forces were able to control the organization of the convention. For example, when Huey Long and, in Flynn's words, "his little army," marched into Flynn's hotel room at two a.m. one morning pledging support for Roosevelt, Long could assume that the credentials committee would vote to seat his delegation and not a rival one from Louisiana. Later at the convention, on the fourth and final ballot, Long prevailed on the Arkansas and Mississippi delegations to hold for Roosevelt. As Flynn put it, "There is no question in my mind but that without Long's work Roosevelt might not have been nominated." Ironically, it would not be long before Long would become one of Roosevelt's most serious political adversaries.

Another key to Roosevelt's fourth-ballot victory was the move of California (initially for its own Senator William

McAdoo and heavily influenced by William Randolph Hearst) and Texas (initially for house Speaker John Garner, a native son) to Roosevelt. Because Garner ended up as the vice presidential nominee, many assumed that a deal had been made. Flynn denied this. Roosevelt "was never a man to work a deal involving political preferment."

Garner's selection was actually a defeat for Flynn, who, in his own words, "was very much opposed to Garner's nomination." Flynn was concerned that Garner might alienate Irish Catholics "who were by tradition mostly Democratic" and who blamed the south, and particularly Texas, for not supporting Smith in 1928. Roosevelt decided on Garner after participating in a long conference call with Flynn, Howe, Farley and others at the convention, and recognizing that the Texan would add southern support to the ticket. In Flynn's words, Garner was the "most available" possibility. Later Flynn would admit that he was wrong to oppose the selection. He wrote, "Garner was named as his running mate on the basis of what Roosevelt thought the situation demanded. Circumstances proved he was right."

The big loser at the Chicago convention—certainly in his own mind—was Smith. He could not bring himself to concede, insisting on remaining a candidate to the very end and refusing to support a motion to make the nomination unanimous at the conclusion of balloting. As various accounts confirm, Smith left the convention a bitter man, slipping out a side door after the final vote and immediately boarding a train to New York. It took him five days to publicly support the ticket, and he was essentially absent for the fall campaign. For the rest of his life, he wanted nothing to do with either Flynn or Roosevelt. In fact, according to Elizabeth Perry, the granddaughter of his longtime advisor Belle Moskowitz, Smith "swore and raged" whenever Roosevelt's name came up. After

Malcolm MacKay

King Edward VII and Queen Elizabeth at the New York World's Fair (1939), Flynn at far left.

Flynn with FDR's mother, 1939, at the New York World's Fair.

From left to right: FDR, La Guardia, Eleanor Roosevelt and Flynn.

FDR and Flynn, 1932.
(Note Roosevelt's leg brace below pant leg.)

Helen and Ed Flynn with children.
(left to right: Sheila, Patrick and Richard.)

Flynn age 50.

the 1932 convention, Mrs. Smith refused to speak to Helen Flynn, although they had been friends.

Historians have long been fascinated by Smith. Kevin Murphy, in *Al Smith and the Fall of Tammany Hall*, deals with the inevitable tension between Smith's two roles: progressive reformer and loyal machine politician. Paula Eldot, in *Governor Al Smith: The Politician as Reformer*, concludes that Smith "was not receptive to progressivism when it threatened the political machine. In case of conflict between the two, loyalty to the party stood higher in his scale of values."

For the next 12 years, Smith served as president of the Empire State Building and spoke increasingly against the New Deal. As the Axis threat grew in the late 1930s, he became a leading isolationist. Murphy describes him as declining into self-pity, and noted columnist Walter Lippmann wrote that Smith's "hatred and resentment and personal frustration are almost overwhelming." Lippmann found Smith to be "an awful human spectacle" suffering from "what almost amounts to a persecution complex." Living near Central Park, he was given a key to the zoo by Robert Moses, and he would spend long hours by himself observing the animals. He died in 1944.

Before Roosevelt could begin his presidential campaign, he had to deal with two pressing questions back home: whom should the party nominate to succeed him as governor, and what should be done about Jimmy Walker, the city's high-living mayor? In both cases, Roosevelt was acutely sensitive to the fact that in answering these questions, he might further alienate the old-line party regulars whose support he needed in the presidential election.

Just as Smith had wanted the strongest possible New York ticket in 1928 to help him carry the state in the presidential election, now Roosevelt wanted the same in 1932. The obvious choice for governor was Herbert Lehman, heir to a family

fortune, party loyalist and lieutenant governor under
Roosevelt. He would also be the state's first Jewish governor.
The old line party bosses—Tammany's Curry, Brooklyn's
McCooey, Albany's O'Connell—were not so keen. They saw
Lehman as too independent, at least from them. He had
supported Roosevelt over Smith at the convention and worked
closely with Flynn, whom the other bosses resented as
Roosevelt's close ally and chief patronage dispenser.

The unhappy bosses had a plan: get Senator Robert Wagner,
who would become the most important advocate of the New
Deal legislation in the senate, to give up his seat and run for
governor, with Lehman becoming the party's senate candidate.
Governors have more patronage positions to offer than senators
and the bosses thought they would have more influence with
Wagner.

At the behest of both Roosevelt and Lehman, Flynn
organized the successful effort against the proposed candidate
switch, including a public relations campaign in favor of
Lehman for governor directed at the increasingly influential
Jewish electorate. At the state Democratic convention Lehman
was nominated by Roosevelt and seconded by Smith. Both
Lehman and Wagner went on to win their respective elections.
Lehman would be reelected governor three times and then
succeed Wagner as senator. Flynn later described Lehman's
1932 nomination as "an example of how public opinion can
compel party bosses to accede to the wishes of the rank and
file majority. It proves that bosses can be beaten. They can be
beaten when they go against what the people want."

There remained the problem posed by Jimmy Walker, a
problem, as earlier noted, Flynn had helped create by leading
the effort to replace Mayor Hylan with Walker in 1925.
Walker was a much beloved figure in New York café society,
and emblematic of the city high life during the roaring

twenties. As Flynn later admitted, he was blinded by Beau James' "quickness and great personal charm ... ."

It became increasingly evident, particularly after Walker's reelection victory over Republican fusion candidate Fiorello LaGuardia in 1929, that his administration was tolerating a significant level of corruption. While always maintaining—at least publicly—that Walker was personally honest, Flynn came to recognize that "many of the people who surrounded Walker were superficial and rapacious. He found it hard to believe that any of his friends were bad or even wrong." Flynn also recognized that, while he may not have consciously accepted bribes, "Walker and his family were the recipients of numerous 'beneficences.' " Flynn once described Walker as "not a person who looked very deeply into anything." As noted by Robert Caro, the biographer of Robert Moses, "The Mayor personally accepted more than a million dollars from firms doing business with the city."

Beginning in 1930, Judge Samuel Seabury conducted a series of investigations of the city government that raised serious questions about Walker and his administration. Perhaps one bit of testimony best captures what Seabury uncovered. The judge asked one of Walker's appointees how, with a city salary of $12,000 a year, he had, in just a seven-year period, savings of $396,000. The answer was that the large amount came from "monies that I had saved" in a tin box. "Kind of a magic box?" Seabury inquired. "It was a wonderful box," came the reply.

Under state law, the governor had the authority to remove the mayor for cause. It fell to Roosevelt, after he had received the Democratic presidential nomination, to conduct a public hearing on the question of Walker's possible removal. Walker did poorly at the hearing, and there was little his allies could do to help his cause. As he commented, "There are things a man must do alone—be born, die and testify." On September 1, before Roosevelt had made his decision, Walker resigned. He had been told by Smith that he had no choice. Roosevelt was thus spared having to remove Walker.

The Seabury investigations, while searching for corruption in all the city's counties, found little in the Bronx. There was a magistrate who discussed with a district leader a case before him involving a client of the leader. Questions were also raised about some real estate manipulations by the Bronx commissioner of public works, appointed long before Flynn assumed his party position. Flynn himself was investigated, and later wrote, "Judge Seabury and his assistants examined me many times and went thoroughly into every phase of my life. They were invited to look at the books of my law firm, and they exhaustively examined my bank accounts and those of my family. Nothing was ever found. There was nothing wrong to find."

Looking back years later, Flynn had mixed emotions about the Seabury investigations. He was proud that the Bronx emerged with a relatively clean reputation. To quote, "The most promising candidate for public office sometimes turns out to be weak. There has not been an administration in American history, whether city, county, state, or federal, that did not have its 'margin of error.' When I compare the findings of the Seabury investigation in Bronx County with its findings in the four [other city counties], I am satisfied that mine is not only the most businesslike, but also the safest system."

Still, the Seabury experience left Flynn with considerable bitterness: "When the entire proceeding was finished and I asked him [Seabury] to issue a statement saying that he had been offered an opportunity to examine the law firm, my family and me fully, he declined to do it. This is something men in the public eye have to reckon with: although they are personally cleared of charges, the persons making the charges, whether officials or newspapers, seldom have the decency to withdraw them when they find they are not true."

15 TO THE WHITE HOUSE

After the excitement of Roosevelt's nomination, the actual election seemed almost anticlimactic. Although Flynn worried in early 1932 that Republican incumbent Herbert Hoover might be a strong candidate, events during the year, including growing unemployment that reached 24 percent by the November election, worked in favor of the challenger. Roosevelt's campaign was largely policy free, and he attacked Hoover as much from the right as the left: "I accuse the present Administration of being the greatest spending Administration in peace time in our history." Vice presidential candidate Garner went even further, describing Hoover as "leading the country down the path of socialism."

Farley replaced Raskob as chairman of the national party, and became campaign manager. Flynn and Howe set up travel itineraries, while "the brain trust" of academics and professionals organized by Professor Raymond Moley of Columbia worked on speeches and policy. As he had for the 1928 election, Flynn took particular responsibility for New York. He also accompanied Roosevelt to California, where the Democratic Party was riven with conflicts and had little real organization.

As the campaign progressed, Flynn found it "obvious to everyone" that Roosevelt would win and gave high marks to Eleanor Roosevelt, Jim Farley, Louis Howe, and, most of all, the candidate himself. It was an overwhelming victory, 42 states (including the entire south) to six (four from New England plus Delaware and New Jersey). The popular vote percentages were 57 percent to 40. Nineteen thirty-two would be the last time the Republican Party would carry the African-American vote in a presidential election. Flynn believed that "the birth of the New Deal actually occurred during the many conferences in Chicago [at the convention], where 'the marriage' between certain conservative southern Democrats and progressive Democrats in the north and west took place."

Immediately after the election, a small group—Flynn, Howe, Farley and Frank Walker, the businessman who served as treasurer of the presidential campaign—formed to advise the president-elect on federal appointments for key campaign supporters, particularly those in the category FRBC, For Roosevelt Before Chicago. Among the FRBC supporters were Joseph E. Davis (appointed ambassador to Russia), Cordell Hull (secretary of state), Joseph P. Kennedy (chairman of the Securities and Exchange Commission) and Henry Morgenthau, Jr. (several positions ending with the secretary of the treasury). Roosevelt asked Flynn to become collector of customs for the port of New York, but Flynn decided to stay on as New York's secretary of state in Governor Lehman's administration. He also decided to continue as Democratic national committeeman for New York and chairman of the Bronx party. Alan Nevins, a Lehman biographer, described Flynn, who served in the Lehman administration until 1939, as "a confidante and mainstay" to the governor who "was as useful for his general ideas as for his hardboiled political advice. He remained a versatile and thoughtful man, who helped modify the excessive seriousness that sometimes made Lehman too tense for his own good."

Roosevelt hadn't given up on Flynn. While the latter was visiting the White House on an overnight trip, soon after the inauguration, the president told him after dinner, "I want you down here in the United States Senate." Royal Copeland, who—along with Robert Wagner—represented New York in the senate, was rumored to be unhappy in Washington, or at least his wife was unhappy. A Tammany Democrat, Copeland was not a Roosevelt favorite, and was up for re-election in 1934. Roosevelt had the idea of appointing Copeland ambassador to Germany, and then asking Lehman to appoint Flynn to fill the vacancy. Flynn discussed the possibility with Lehman, who was happy to make the appointment but believed that he had an obligation to offer it first to former Governor Smith. Flynn then had several conversations with Smith, who equivocated and wouldn't come to a decision. As Flynn put it, "It was apparent as I talked to Smith that the sores and hurts made at the convention had not yet been healed." With Smith keeping everyone waiting, the opportunity was lost. Copeland ran successfully for reelection the next year.

Roosevelt had yet another idea for Flynn: ambassador to Germany (where Hitler had become chancellor in January 1933). After discussing the offer with Helen and not wanting to disrupt the lives of their small children, Flynn declined. The man who did get the ambassadorship was William F. Dodd, a professor of American history at the University of Chicago who had written extensively about the American south. He became known to some people, including Flynn, as "telephone book" Dodd because they believed Roosevelt had intended to appoint a different Dodd. This second Dodd, Walter F., was a distinguished lawyer and professor of political science at the University of Illinois. Ambassador William F. Dodd served with distinction in Germany during the early Hitler years. His daughter Martha, as described by Erik Larson in *In the Garden of Beasts*, had romantic relations with several leading Nazi figures and went on to become a Soviet spy.

After the elections, Professor Moley continued as the organizing force behind the "brain trust" of academics and others who provided the policymaking behind the New Deal. Flynn, Farley and Moley worked well together while maintaining a clear distinction between politics and policy. In Flynn's words, "We attempted to keep a strict differentiation between the job of organizing and that of policymaking ... . " During the first term, virtually all appointees were connected with Democratic Party organizations. By the second term, Roosevelt felt less constrained by the need to please the party machines, recognizing that the party needed him as much as he needed it. As Flynn observed, "The machine remained loyal to him. This can be understood when it is remembered that the business of the political machine is to elect candidates. The Roosevelt name was magic throughout the country... he provided them [the bosses] with power that had nothing to do with federal appointments. His prestige enabled them to elect their local candidates and thus keep in power."

Political machines live off patronage, and the New Deal presented them with a job bonanza. The civil service reforms of the late 19th and early 20th centuries had taken many jobs, at all levels of government, away from the party bosses. With the New Deal, patronage appointments made a comeback. The Federal Emergency Relief Act of 1933 declared that the positions created by the emergency relief agencies were "exempt" from civil service. Thus the public works programs of the New Deal, including the Works Progress Administration run by Harry Hopkins, became major employers, with Hopkins and other program administrators, despite denials, looking to party organizations for recruits. As economist and columnist Paul Krugman put it, "For while he (Hopkins) felt that patronage and nepotism had no place in personnel management, he was convinced that one of the crucial skills of the public administrator was an ability to engage in the political arena to sell a program to the Congress and to the public." Among many New York projects benefiting from WPA funding were the Eighth Avenue Subway, LaGuardia Airport, the Lincoln and Queens Mid-Town Tunnels, the Triborough Bridge and Brooklyn College.

Hopkins, of course, was an agent of the president. To quote historian Paul Van Riper, "Franklin D. Roosevelt fully understood the intricate relationship of party, program and patronage ... Roosevelt rewarded and punished to support his social program and to bind together the discordant party he had inherited." As Roosevelt's favorite boss and Lehman's secretary of state, Flynn was the man to see in New York. He actually served for a period as a regional administrator for the National Recovery Administration, with a budget of $3.3 billion for projects in New York, New Jersey and Pennsylvania. It soon became necessary, however, to share some of this patronage power with—of all people—a Republican: Fiorello La Guardia.

16 LA GUARDIA

The split within the Democratic Party between the Roosevelt and Smith factions, so evident at the 1932 national convention, reappeared at the state convention that nominated Lieutenant Governor Herbert Lehman to succeed Roosevelt as governor, and then again in a bitter fight over control of New York City Hall. When Jimmy Walker resigned as mayor in the late summer of 1932, he was succeeded—on an interim basis—by Joseph V. McKee, president of the board of aldermen. Universally respected and known as "Honest Joe" and even "Holy Joe," McKee was a former public school teacher and Fordham law graduate who had come up through the Bronx Democratic organization. Starting as a state assemblyman in 1918—the good- government group Citizens Union concluded that he "did himself and his constituency credit"—he became president of the city's board of aldermen seven years later. Running for reelection in 1929, he got more votes than Walker running for mayor. Flynn now wanted the party to support McKee in a special mayoral election in November to select someone to complete the one year remaining in Walker's term.

McKee, had he received the Democratic nomination, would have easily won the special election. In his brief time as acting mayor he showed great promise, supporting various fiscal and political reforms including the reduction of his own salary. His problem was that the mayor's office was a significant source of patronage and the other county bosses weren't about to concede control of such patronage to Flynn. This was particularly true of the Tammany leader, John Curry, who had none of Charles Murphy's vision and sense of purpose. While Tammany was not as dominant within the city's Democratic Party as it had been—after all, by 1930 the Brooklyn population was 2.6 million and the Bronx 1.2 million, with Manhattan only 1.9 million—Curry was able to unite all the county leaders except Flynn behind a surrogate court judge named John Patrick O'Brien. O'Brien was, as one commentator described him, "a genial bumbler."

At the city Democratic convention to nominate a mayoral candidate for the special election, Flynn realized that McKee couldn't win, and so, in the name of party unity, he agreed to second O'Brien's nomination. Years later, Flynn recalled, "This was the one time in my life when I did not remain true to what I actually believed. Plainly my action in seconding the nomination of O'Brien was a mistake. I should have followed my own best judgment instead of listening to my friends … (who) believed that the first consideration was to remain 'regular'… that it is more important to be regular than to be right. I have never subscribed to that theory. And as I departed from it [being right rather than regular] in this instance, I can only say that I have regretted it."

O'Brien was elected in the special election, although McKee got almost a quarter of a million write-in votes. A year later McKee declined to challenge the incumbent mayor for the Democratic nomination, and O'Brien became the party's candidate in the 1933 regular election. Meanwhile, a fusion collection of Republicans, disaffected Democrats and others came together to back a liberal Republican who had been defeated in the 1929 mayoral election and for reelection to Congress in the Roosevelt landslide of 1932. Not your usual

Republican reformer, he was Fiorello La Guardia, an Episcopalian with a Jewish mother and an Italian-American father. As described by Robert Moses, "The Mayor [La Guardia] adopted a Lincolnesque approach to Harlem, made broad his phylacteries in East New York, emphasized his ancestral links with an unquestionable respect for the Roman Catholic Church, and attended an occasional Church of England service at St John's Cathedral . [If the city had a] solid group of Chinese Mohemmedens, he would doubtless have discovered strong ties with them."

Flynn recognized that La Guardia could play the game. "Possibly outside of President Roosevelt and Governor Smith," he wrote, "La Guardia is the smartest politician I have ever met in my political career." By summer's end 1933, a victory of La Guardia over O'Brien was looking possible.

Down in Washington, Roosevelt was worried. An O'Brien win would play to the advantage of the worst elements of the New York Democratic organization, still resentful of Smith's defeat a year earlier. On the other hand, a La Guardia victory would weaken the Democratic Party in its heartland. It was time to invite Flynn to the White House, which Roosevelt did in mid-September. The president asked Flynn to lead an effort to get McKee to run for mayor as a third-party candidate. A McKee victory would give the city—in effect—a Democratic administration with whom the White House could work.

After considerable hesitation, McKee succumbed to Flynn's pleadings and agreed to run. Flynn organized the formation of the Recovery Party and attracted a number of prominent New Yorkers—many Democrats—to the effort. *The Literary Digest*, later famous for wrongly predicting that Alf Landon would beat Roosevelt in 1936, conducted a poll that indicated that McKee would win the three-cornered race.

Victory seemed increasingly possible, but then, ten days
before the election, La Guardia accused McKee of anti-
semitism. The charge was based on a sentence, taken out of
context, in an article McKee had written for *The Catholic World*
eighteen years earlier. Samuel Untermyer, a leading figure in
the Jewish community and a McKee supporter, switched to La
Guardia. A number of other prominent Jewish leaders did as
well, or at least retracted their support for McKee.

In response, McKee tried to show that, as Flynn put it, "His
entire life was a story of tolerance." Meanwhile, Flynn urged
Roosevelt, who had maintained neutrality in public, to make
an endorsement. As was so often true in these situations,
however, Roosevelt protected his political capital and remained
silent. Earlier in the mayoral campaign, when White House
aide Adolf Berle, a La Guardia supporter, had tried to persuade
the president to ask Flynn to convince McKee to withdraw,
Roosevelt replied that he had no control over Flynn. La
Guardia won with 40 percent of the vote, with McKee second
with 28. Herbert Bayard Swope, the well-known New York
newspaperman and a McKee supporter, summed up the
feelings of the McKee camp: "We had the best candidate, we
had the best leaders, and we had the best arguments. But the
people would not believe us."

For the rest of his life Flynn would look back at the La
Guardia election with bitterness. For one thing, there was Roy
Howard, chairman of Scripps-Howard and publisher of *The
World Telegram*, an influential evening paper. Howard, whom
Flynn later described as "personally as vain as any bantam
rooster," had committed to supporting McKee, but then
switched to La Guardia and, in Flynn's description, became
"violently opposed to McKee." Flynn felt betrayed, and—on a
train to Albany after the election—the two men had an
argument that ended with lots of shouting. To quote Flynn,

"In language that was very crisp and sometimes profane, I told him what I thought of his actions. I did not mince words." In the ensuing years, Flynn would find himself the subject of attacks and "investigations" by *The World Telegram*. The paper was instrumental in defeating Roosevelt's nomination of Flynn in 1943 to a major diplomatic post.

Bad as Howard was in Flynn's view during the 1933 mayoral campaign, La Guardia himself was even worse. Flynn thought the successful candidate's attacks on McKee for anti-semitism were completely unfair, and La Guardia himself later admitted, "I invented a low blow." Flynn also blamed La Guardia for encouraging what we would now call the Mafia to use strong-arm tactics in the campaign. The truth appears to be that elements of organized crime supported La Guardia, but without the knowledge or encouragement of the candidate.

What most bothered Flynn about La Guardia may have been the latter's hypocrisy concerning party organizations. "He used Tammany Hall and the 'boss system' as whipping boys. Yet he himself set up one of the best political machines that ever functioned in New York." Flynn objected to La Guardia's repeated use of the term "spoils system," implying "wrong doing if not downright dishonesty" and "... that all the evils of government could be traced to it." As Flynn saw it, La Guardia appointed to public office his supporters almost exclusively, and worked hard to build a rival patronage organization.

The 1933 mayoral election result complicated Flynn's life, but it also offered him great opportunity. With a friend in the White House and another, Governor Lehman, in Albany, and no fellow Democrat in city hall, he emerged as the unchallenged Democratic patronage chief in the city. Also, unlike what happened elsewhere in the city during the election, in the Bronx, by Flynn's order, all Democratic local candidates also ran with Recovery Party endorsement, and thus all won. The Democratic Party was in total control of the Bronx, and Flynn, of the party. The complication was that, while Flynn was the pre-eminent Democratic boss in town, Roosevelt recognized the value of good relations with the new mayor. La Guardia became very much a member of the coalition of New Deal supporters in New York, and endorsed Roosevelt in the three presidential elections that occurred while he was mayor. In 1940, he said he preferred Roosevelt with his "known faults" to Willkie with his "unknown virtues." In return, the city became the recipient of a disproportionate amount of federal money and programs, and Flynn had to share with the mayor some of the resulting patronage. Flynn also was careful to say nice things about La Guardia in public. For example, *The New York Times* reported on March 30, 1941: "Speaking at Chapel Hill, North Carolina, Democratic boss Edward Flynn called La Guardia 'one of the best mayors that New York ever had.' "

Privately Flynn expressed mixed views on La Guardia. He found him "an honest man ... [with] a real desire to give a good administration to the city." Yet he also said of this supposedly honest man, "No one in the United States has a better knowledge of political tricks than La Guardia. No one ever used those tricks more unscrupulously."

The Flynn-LaGuardia dance began as soon as the new mayor entered City Hall. The mayor proposed state legislation that would give him the power to reduce city expenses by eliminating jobs and consolidating departments. Many regular Democrats saw this as an attack on city workers and a way for La Guardia to enhance his patronage powers. The city's legislators in Albany were strongly opposed. Behind the scenes, Flynn led a compromise effort. Reporters knew the compromise would succeed when James Lyons, the Bronx borough president and very much a Flynn protégé, came out in its favor.

La Guardia maintained his anti-boss reputation throughout his mayoralty. He presented himself as being of no party, or maybe above all parties. Still, he could work with Flynn, sometimes at a personal cost. For example, Flynn, believing that Jimmy Walker was personally honest "in his fashion" and in need of employment, asked La Guardia—just days before the mayor endorsed Roosevelt for reelection in 1940—to find a city job for Walker. La Guardia did so, word got out, and he was completely taken aback by the criticism that ensued. While visiting Detroit, he was asked by a reporter, "Are you still taking orders from Boss Flynn?" The mayor grabbed the reporter's tie and tore his collar, and others separated the two men.

In the spring of 1941 La Guardia was preparing to run for a third term. Adolf Berle, close to both the mayor and the president, asked Flynn if La Guardia could receive the Democratic Party endorsement. Flynn replied, "The boys (party leaders) wouldn't stand for it." The mayor went on to a resounding victory over a strong Democratic candidate, William O'Dwyer, the Brooklyn district attorney.

A referendum passed as part of the 1941 mayoral election eliminating county registrars and sheriffs and creating in their place two citywide offices. Flynn asked La Guardia if he could save four Bronx county employees from job elimination by converting their patronage jobs to civil service. According to La Guardia biographer Thomas Kessner, the mayor went along with Flynn because he wanted to stay on Roosevelt's good side. The chairman of the city's civil service commission objected to the plan. *The World Telegram* sided with the chairman. Ultimately the courts affirmed the legality of the mayor's action, but both La Guardia and Flynn received serious criticism. More importantly, in covering the story, the press picked up another story about paving blocks installed in the driveway of Flynn's country place that will be discussed in a later chapter.

Two more situations involving Flynn and La Guardia occurred in early 1943. Flynn's ambassadorial nomination (also discussed later) came before the senate's foreign affairs committee. La Guardia was asked to testify, and this is part of what he said: "I cannot qualify as a character witness [for Flynn] because of the bitterness that has existed for years between us and because of my prejudice against him." As Kessner pointed out, "He [La Guardia] had avoided giving aid to Flynn's foes or any cause for resentment by the president. At the same time he had cleared himself of lingering suspicions that he had been a little too close to the Bronx boss."

La Guardia may have been hoisted on his own petard. Although the senate committee approved Flynn's nomination, the candidate withdrew before a full senate vote and amidst lots of bad press concerning his qualifications. Roosevelt, burned by the whole proceeding, decided not to go forward with another appointment he was considering, making La Guardia a brigadier general (he had already been fitted for the uniform) and director of civil affairs in liberated Italy. It was something La Guardia really wanted.

The next year, 1944, Flynn and La Guardia had a confrontation over whether to support increasing the subway fare from five to ten cents. The fare had remained at five cents for over 40 years, and the system was in desperate need of funds. While the politicians, including La Guardia, understood the need for a fare increase, none stepped forward to lead the effort. One historian wrote this about the mayor, "On the subject of the five-cent fare ... La Guardia proved particularly evasive." La Guardia argued that the city and state legislative bodies should come up with a solution, especially because "Republicans have the state legislature. Democrats have the city council." Flynn, who had considerable sway over these legislative bodies, made it clear that he would support a fare increase, but only if the mayor publicly called for it to be enacted. La Guardia ducked, nothing got done and it wasn't until 1948, after La Guardia, that a ten-cent fare was instituted.

17 STAYING HOME

Herbert Lehman's father and two uncles, German immigrants, founded the investment bank Lehman Brothers. Herbert gave up his partnership in the firm when he became lieutenant governor in Roosevelt's state administration. Flynn described Lehman as having "made an excellent record as lieutenant governor. He had divested himself of all his business interests, moved to Albany, and devoted his entire time to the job. It was probably the first time in the history of New York that any man had given full time to that office." Although reserved and, like Flynn, most comfortable in small gatherings, he was elected lieutenant governor twice, governor four times, and U.S. senator in a special election and then for a full term. Flynn found that Roosevelt and Lehman "became very warm friends," as did he with Lehman.

Governor Lehman's administration in New York, sometimes described as "the little New Deal," was known for its reform of the state's purchasing practices, wage and employment laws regarding women and children, comprehensive unemployment relief, public housing initiatives and utility regulation. The state led the country in receiving federal support for various New Deal projects. Shortly before the end of his final term as governor, Lehman resigned to become director general of the United Nations Relief and Rehabilitation Administration.

Although Flynn stayed in New York when Roosevelt decamped for Washington, their close personal relationship continued. While clearly more involved with politics than policy, Flynn found himself involved with both. He later wrote, "I continued to see the President and stayed many times at the White House. We would discuss all of his various problems, and our friendship and close association grew with the years." Roosevelt may have become more dependent on Flynn's friendship and advice after Louis Howe died in the summer of 1936.

Over time, the Roosevelt-Flynn friendship grew to include their wives. The Flynn children used to joke that the reason the family was so often asked to the White House was because the president liked to flirt with their mother. At least one visit, in 1940, included the Flynn's governess. The boys remembered an overnight visit when, waking up early, they explored down a long hallway and entered what they thought was an empty room. In fact, the president was in the room having breakfast in bed. He greeted the boys enthusiastically. He then proceeded to point out a portrait of Grover Cleveland on a wall. "Boys," Patrick recalled him saying, "when I was your age my father took me to the White House to meet President Cleveland. The president gave me some very good advice, never take this job." Roosevelt proceeded to give the Flynn boys the same advice.

18 COURT-PACKING AND PURGES

Starting early in his presidency, Roosevelt voiced his frustrations with the Supreme Court's invalidation of New Deal legislation. The court's actions, Flynn wrote, "nettled him a great deal. He felt that something should be done to prevent the Supreme Court from nullifying the will of the people as expressed by Congress." Still, Roosevelt chose to let the situation ride during his first term.

Called "the campaign without a mistake," the Roosevelt-Garner ticket carried 46 of the 48 states in the 1936 election. On election night, Jim Farley made his famous observation, "As Maine goes, so goes Vermont." Farley was a good campaign manager but Flynn also gave Roosevelt himself lots of credit. If the 1936 victory had a significant downside, it was that it caused Roosevelt to become overconfident, and led directly to his failed attempt to "pack" the Supreme Court with additional justices. The court-packing episode permanently tarnished Roosevelt's reputation.

Although there were hints of what was to come during the 1936 campaign, it wasn't until February 1937 that Roosevelt publicly proposed what became known as the Judicial Procedures Reform Bill. The bill would have granted the president the power to appoint additional justices—up to six—to the Supreme Court for every sitting justice age 70 years 6 months or older. Flynn was dead set against the idea, and he let the president know early exactly where he stood. "I had always been a great believer in the sharply defined functions of the Executive, Judicial, and Legislative branches of our government. I felt that each should remain independent and be free to act, even at the sacrifice of unity. Particularly I did not believe that the Executive should attempt either to dictate or be in a position to dictate his will to the Supreme Court ... I told the President what I believed ... Since I could not agree with him, I was not consulted especially about the plan that he subsequently advocated to reform the Supreme Court."

The court-packing initiative, lead by Thomas Corcoran—Roosevelt called him "Tommy the Cork"—and other brain trusters ended, despite some face-saving legislation, in complete failure. This was of no surprise to many members of Congress. Democrats joined Republicans in opposition. Vice President Garner lobbied quietly against passage, thus beginning his estrangement from the president that would result in his replacement on the 1940 ticket. Another Texan, Sam Rayburn, soon to be speaker of the house, was also opposed, as were several Democratic senators, including the usually pro-New Deal Burton Wheeler. New York's Robert Wagner remained silent.

One historian, Michael Parrish, had this to say about the court-packing escapade: "The protracted legislative battle over the court-packing bill blunted the momentum for additional reforms, divided the New Deal Coalition, squandered the political advantage Roosevelt had gained in the 1936 election and gave fresh ammunition to those who accused him of dictatorship, tyranny and fascism."

Significantly, as 1937 proceeded, the court, under the leadership of Justice Owen Roberts, began its move toward greater acceptance of New Deal initiatives, including specifically those involving the minimum wage, organized labor and business regulation. The court's movement, sometimes described as "the switch in time that saved nine," undercut Roosevelt's court-packing plan. Had he been more patient, he would have solved his court problem—as he eventually did—by appointments to fill court vacancies. In his 12 years plus as president, he appointed eight of the nine justices.

Nineteen thirty-seven was also a year of severe economic downturn—"the recession within the Depression"—with unemployment approaching 20 percent by year's end. Most economists cite as a precipitating cause Roosevelt's decision to reduce spending in an attempt to balance the budget. A few conservative economists blame the tax increase enacted in 1936 and greater unionization of the work force.

In 1938, Roosevelt embarked on a campaign to purge by primary challenges those he called "yes, but" Democrats, who he felt were not sufficiently supportive of his programs. Here is Flynn's description of the purge attempt: "After the defeat of his Court program and to some extent because of the advice of Thomas G. Corcoran, the famous 'purge' of Senators and Congressmen who had opposed him on the Court fight was started. As this program was developed, it was decided more or less to get rid of not only the members of the Senate and the House who had opposed him in the Court battle but also those who had opposed him on legislation he had advanced in Congress." As justification of the purge attempts, Roosevelt had this to say, "I feel that I have every right to speak in these few instances where there may be a clear issue between candidates for a Democratic nomination involving their principles, or involving a clear misuse of my own name."

While Flynn joined Roosevelt in wanting the Democratic Party to become more progressive, he was adamantly opposed to a systematic attack on incumbent congressmen by encouraging primary opposition. He knew it would fail and leave a residue of bitterness. Here is Flynn on his advice to Roosevelt: "Again I had a talk with him and told him I did not believe in the idea of the 'purge.' I told him he was entirely wrong in attempting to go into the various states to defeat Senators who had not supported the legislation he wanted. I felt he could not win in the long run because the people of the states would resent his interference. Clearly in the end he would come out the worse from such an adventure and with impaired influence and prestige. Again, my opinion was not followed."

Three senate primaries with incumbents seeking re-election were targeted by the White House: Maryland (incumbent Millard Tydings), Georgia (Walter George), and South Carolina ("Cotton Ed" Smith). These three incumbents had opposed Roosevelt on court-packing and other New Deal legislative initiatives. Just as Flynn had predicted, the purge attempts failed in every instance. The pro-New Deal challengers were portrayed as post-Reconstruction carpetbaggers and enemies of states' rights.

Most historians have seen the failure of the purge attempt as a serious defeat for Roosevelt. Arthur Schlesinger Jr. called it "an almost complete failure." Alan Brinkley wrote that the purge "offended the regional pride of both liberal and conservative Democrats in the region (the south)." It certainly served as a harbinger of the flagging ties between the northern and southern wings of the Democratic Party. One pro-Roosevelt cartoon depicted the southern Democrats as a ball and chain hobbling the party's forward movement.

Virtually all the party's other bosses agreed with Flynn and distanced themselves from the purge effort. The same was true—privately - of Jim Farley, chairman of the Democratic national committee, except when it came to Millard Tydings, whom he detested. Even Flynn made an exception to his purge opposition, agreeing to Roosevelt's request that he lead a campaign to unseat Representative John J. O'Conner of New York. O'Conner, as chairman of the house rules committee, had opposed many New Deal regulatory and tax initiatives. Flynn strongly disliked him. With the active participation of WPA workers, Flynn's candidate, James Fay, won both the primary against O'Conner and the general election. In fact, the Fay victory was the purge initiative's only electoral success.

The 1938 congressional elections saw substantial gains by the Republicans. They added 81 seats in the house, almost doubling their previous total of 86. In the senate they went from 15 to 23. Farley, after conferring with party leaders across the country, let go at Corcoran and his White House allies: "I trace all the woes of the Democratic Party, directly and indirectly, to this interference in purely local affairs. In any political entity, voters naturally and rightfully resent the unwarranted invasion of outsiders." Adolf Berle, an original member of the brain trust who went on to hold several important positions in the Roosevelt administration, called Corcoran "a corrupt progressive—he had a good deal of the Irish Fenian about him, and the law meant very little." Senator Wagner told his assistant, Leon Keyserling, "Don't have anything to do with that fellow Corcoran. I don't want to see him around the office."

19 JAMES FARLEY

As previously noted, Flynn, not wanting either assignment himself, supported Roosevelt's choice of Jim Farley to manage the 1932 presidential campaign and succeed Raskob as national chairman of the Democratic Party. Farley would serve as party chairman through Roosevelt's first two terms, and also postmaster general for most of this time. He saw himself as an organizer of the political machinery, and not a policy maker. He wrote: "No one ever charged me with being the big 'inside man,' and I certainly never tried to take over the role. Banking and financial problems were unfamiliar to me, and so were a number of other very complex matters that had to be considered and legislated in a hurry."

Farley himself was complex—a good manager, personable, ambitious, and socially insecure. In his 1938 memoir *Behind the Ballots: The Personal History of a Politician*, he wrote about advising the president in their frequent meetings on public attitudes, political issues and federal patronage. Most of the time, Farley's—and really the party's—recommended candidates for federal judges, U.S. marshals, federal attorneys and other positions were accepted by Roosevelt. According to Farley, however, "The President goes into each case with extreme care. Very often I bring out the name of the person recommended, and he says at once, 'not big enough for the job.' "

After the 1936 election victory, Farley began discussing with various prominent Democrats whom the party should nominate in 1940. Everyone assumed Roosevelt would not run for a third term, something no one had ever done. Many who talked to Farley got the distinct impression that he was interested in being considered himself. As far as Flynn could determine, Farley never talked to Roosevelt about his ambition, but word got back to the president. He was not pleased. As Flynn noted, "Because Farley was really, although not openly, campaigning for either the Presidency or the Vice Presidency a certain coolness had developed between him and the President."

While Roosevelt and Farley did not themselves discuss the latter's presidential ambition, the president did ask Flynn to encourage Farley to run for governor of New York in 1938. Governor Lehman had voiced a desire to retire, and Roosevelt, according to Flynn, believed "it was a mistake for Farley to aspire to either of the offices [president or vice president] without first creating a background of statesmanship. His reputation had been earned through his political activities. He had not been directly connected with the forming of public policies. He had no public record other than a short service in the New York State legislature. As State Chairman of the Democratic Committee in New York and as National Chairman, it had been his function to carry on political organization and to observe neutrality with respect to policies on which, in many instances, there were differences of opinion within the party."

Farley had no interest in running for governor in 1938 and felt betrayed by Roosevelt when the latter accepted the party's nomination for a third term two years later. Upon Roosevelt's renomination in 1940, Farley resigned as party chairman. He refused to campaign for the ticket, although he did indicate—

as he would again in 1944—that he would vote Democratic. He later claimed that "had it not been for the man [Roosevelt] many have credited me with putting in the White House I might have been Vice President or even President."

In his 1938 memoir, Farley had many nice things to say about Roosevelt. He described the president as "the easiest man to do business with I have ever known ... [with] an amazing breadth of ... knowledge about the United States ... a worker, in fact, one of the hardest I have ever known either in business or politics ... one of the strongest men and hardest fighters I have ever known ... humane ... gets such an enormous thrill out of life ... there isn't a snobbish bone in his body... His friends and personal companions are not chosen from any particular group or class." Farley's only criticism of Roosevelt, one he shared with Flynn, was that he avoided firing people who needed to be let go.

In 1948, Farley wrote a second memoir, *Jim Farley's Story: The Roosevelt Years.* The Roosevelt of this book bears little resemblance to the one described earlier. The exciting, inspirational, effective president had become a selfish and disloyal political operative. Farley complained about the power of the White House inner circle, and its interference during the second term with party and patronage matters. While he supported Roosevelt publicly on court-packing, he felt the purge efforts were naïve and counterproductive. To quote Farley, "I knew from the beginning that the purge could lead to nothing but misfortune, because in pursuing his course of vengeance Roosevelt violated a cardinal political creed which demanded that he keep out of local matters."

There was more to Farley's disaffection with Roosevelt than thwarted ambition. As an Irish Catholic working-class high school graduate, he carried a few chips on his shoulders. In complaining that the president did not defend him publicly during an unfair attack by Huey Long, Farley stated, "Apparently I am a bottle of tonic to be taken when needed and then shelved until needed again." He noted that "the President never took me into the bosom of the family" and "I never was invited to spend the night in the historic mansion." In 1938, the Farleys were asked to cruise with the president, and Farley later recalled, "This was the first invitation Mrs. Farley and I had received for a cruise aboard the presidential yacht, although I had been in Washington for more than six years." Farley quoted Eleanor Roosevelt saying, "Franklin finds it hard to relax with people who aren't his social equals."

Joe Kennedy shared some of Farley's social chips when it came to Roosevelt, complaining that the president compartmentalized his associates into social and political friends. Columnist Joseph Alsop speculated about whether Roosevelt's limited success at winning popularity as a young man with his own social set may have led him to look outside it for approval. Although Flynn might occasionally joke about Roosevelt's "Hasty Pudding [a Harvard club] cabinet" of friends aboard Vincent Astor's yacht, on which the president used to cruise, he seems never to have sensed or experienced any condescension or snobbery toward him by the president.

20 THIRD TERM

As noted in the previous chapter, virtually everyone close to Roosevelt, and perhaps even the man himself, assumed that he would not run for a third term. As the international situation deteriorated, Roosevelt began to reconsider. To quote Flynn, "My impression is that sometime early in 1939 his determination began to waiver. He was less emphatic than he previously had been in saying he would not run." Nevertheless, Flynn was "certain that up to April, or perhaps May, of 1940" the president was still undecided. While no loyal Democrat could declare his candidacy for president until Roosevelt publicly took himself out of the race, Roosevelt nevertheless encouraged several men to consider running. Of course the more candidates there were, the less chance any one of them had to succeed.

Harry Hopkins, Jimmy Byrnes, and Cordell Hull were three men Roosevelt encouraged to consider becoming candidates. As a New Deal program administrator and then secretary of commerce, Hopkins was known as a strong supporter of racial equality, creating a problem with southern Democrats. He was divorced and there were also serious questions about his health. Byrnes, a governor and senator from South Carolina, had his own political issues, including a poor civil rights record and his leaving the Catholic Church. Cordell Hull, the secretary of state and former Tennessee congressman and senator, was Farley's favorite 1940 presidential candidate other than himself. Farley, while continuing as party chairman, gave up serving as postmaster general in 1938 to run Coca Cola International. He became known for negotiating favorable contracts with the government that gave Coca Cola special status with the armed forces during World War II. In fact, it was shipped during the war at government expense as a "war priority item" along with food and ammunition.

Beginning early in 1939, voices began to be raised in favor of a third term. Interior Secretary Harold Ickes publicly stated his belief that Roosevelt was "the only man capable of carrying on the liberal tradition who can be nominated and elected." Chicago party boss Ed Kelly called for a draft Roosevelt movement, and he was joined by several other party leaders. Foreign relations and military preparedness took over the national agenda. In October 1939, Roosevelt succeeded in convincing Congress—with southern Democratic and some east coast Republican support—to repeal the Neutrality Act, thereby allowing the allies to purchase American armaments. Prominent Republicans Henry Stimson and Frank Knox joined the cabinet as secretaries of war and navy respectively.

Flynn was not one of those encouraging Roosevelt to run. To quote, "I refrained from urging Roosevelt to attempt another campaign. My early reasons for wishing that the President would retire after two terms were not based on any feeling that he had suffered any loss of popularity. I was not thinking of the political situation but of him as a personal friend. I had seen him during the seven years of his Presidency age considerably under the weight of his great responsibilities. It was obvious to me even then that the President's health was beginning to suffer. I felt that he had done more than his part for the people of the United States."

While unwilling to challenge Roosevelt as long as he remained a possible candidate for re-election, several party bosses were unhappy with him. Their displeasure resulted from the president's increasing tendency to go outside the regular party organizations in making federal appointments. The party men, to quote Flynn, resented others receiving "the patronage to which they (the regulars) felt entitled." Flynn continued, "If the President had continued to appoint Democrats and, in many instances organization Democrats, there would have been no serious opposition in the party to a third-term nomination ... Organization Democrats could very truthfully say that the President had deserted them in favor of the group know as New Dealers. All of this was ammunition for Farley."

As 1940 proceeded and time grew closer for the Democratic convention in Chicago in July, the questions of whether Roosevelt would run and how the third-term issue would play out grew ever larger. Farley and Vice President Garner came out against a third term. Most other prominent Democrats were quiet. Flynn described the situation: "I think it is only fair to say that ...(party leaders) felt that if they did not go along [with whatever Roosevelt decided] the party would be so hopelessly divided that no candidate would have a chance of winning."

By the spring of 1940 Roosevelt clearly wanted to be re-nominated, but he also wanted the whole process to appear as a draft. Publicly he was all reluctance. The Saturday before the convention, he went for a cruise on the presidential yacht with his aide Sam Rosenman, his assistant Missy LeHand, his doctor and two friends. According to Rosenman, "One would never have imagined that significant political history was being made by the calm, thoughtful man sitting in the stern playing with his stamps or reading the paper."

Meanwhile, in Chicago, Flynn, Hopkins, Byrnes and Chicago's Ed Kelly were hard at work securing the renomination. *Time* magazine dubbed the group "the Janizariat" after the sultan's legendary palace guard. While Flynn thought highly of Hopkins—"invariably when I called on him to do anything in Washington, he would get it done,"—he also recognized that Hopkins' presence at the convention was a negative. To quote Flynn, "There was bitterness among the organization leaders at his presence there. While they had nothing against him personally, in fact a great many of them were fond of him, they felt that he, representing the President, distinctly lowered their own prestige." Flynn, seen by the party leaders as one of their own, kept close to Hopkins, "I was with him continuously, offering whatever helpful advice I could."

It was obvious to everyone that, should he decide to run for a third term, Roosevelt had a majority of delegates. The reason, to quote Farley, was simple: "They [the party bosses] all felt that if the President was at the head of the ticket they would get votes for their local ticket." Still many delegates at the convention were unhappy, confused by Roosevelt's apparent indecisiveness, and worried about renewed Republican strength and whether the third-term issue might hurt the ticket. As Secretary of Labor Frances Perkins told Roosevelt over the phone from the convention, "The situation is just as sour as can be."

On Tuesday evening of the convention, Roosevelt decided it was time to inform the delegates that, while they should feel free to vote as they wished, he was available to be drafted. Senator Alben Barkley of Kentucky conveyed the message: "The President has never had and has not today any desire to or purpose to continue in the office of President, to be a candidate for that office, or be nominated by the convention for that office. He wishes in all conviction and sincerity to make it clear that all of the delegates are free to vote for any candidate."

What was clear was that any candidate could be Roosevelt. After Barkley spoke, and thanks to Ed Kelly, a loud voice broadcast repeatedly over the public address system, "We want Roosevelt." The speaker was the Chicago superintendent of sewers, holing up in the convention hall basement, microphone in hand. Roosevelt won overwhelmingly on the first ballot, with Farley, Garner and Tydings garnering a small number of votes.

Who should succeed Garner, who had alienated Roosevelt and taken himself out of consideration for the vice-presidential nomination? There were several discussions among Roosevelt, Flynn, Kelly, Jersey City boss Frank Hague, longtime party loyalist Frank Walker and several others. The consensus candidate was Henry Wallace, of whom Flynn later had this to say: "During my service as United States Commissioner of the New York World's Fair [a largely ceremonial 1939-40 presidential appointment], I had become very friendly with Henry Wallace, the Secretary of Agriculture. He impressed me as being a loyal supporter of the President and of the things for which the President stood. He had been a good administrator of the Department of Agriculture and had brought to the President a certain strength among the farmers."

Wallace was not a popular choice on the convention floor. As Flynn later recalled, "He had no political background whatever. His acquaintance with political leaders was very slight. I was probably the only political leader throughout the country with whom he had been friendly. The rest of the leaders were not in a happy frame of mind. They were sullen and resentful, a feeling accentuated by the fact that Wallace had originally been a Republican who had changed his politics as late as 1932." It didn't help that Wallace had something of a reputation for being a mystic. He described himself as "a searcher for methods of bringing the inner light to outward manifestation and raising outward manifestation to the inner light."

Roosevelt became adamant, letting it be known that he would not run if Wallace was not on the ticket. Flynn worked the delegates, and helped convince Eleanor Roosevelt—a very popular figure among party activists—to speak on Wallace's behalf. Wallace was nominated on the first ballot with 627 votes, only 76 more than needed. Although it was then after midnight, Roosevelt decided to accept his own nomination by radio from Hyde Park, "Lying awake as I have done on many nights, I have asked myself whether I have the right as Commander-in-Chief of the Army and Navy to call on men and women to serve their country ... and at the same time decline to serve my country in my personal capacity if I am called upon to do so by the people of my country."

21 THE 1940 ELECTION

Farley resigned as national party chairman immediately after the convention, and soon thereafter Roosevelt got on the phone. Flynn described his conversation with the president, "Shortly after the convention the president asked me to call and suggested that I take over the office [national party chairman]. I told him that as far as my personal wishes were concerned, I would not under any condition accept the job." Two more conversations followed, and then a call from a Roosevelt aide asking Flynn to come to Hyde Park. Flynn accepted, but finished the conversation by saying, "If it was the chairmanship he wanted to talk about, I wanted to say once more I would not accept it."

As Flynn was leaving his country house to make the trip, his wife Helen warned him not to let "that man" change his mind. At Hyde Park, after lunch with Roosevelt, Hopkins and Walker, Flynn found himself alone with the president: "This was unfortunate for me, because before I left the President had convinced me that I should take the chairmanship. When I returned home Mrs. Flynn met me at the door. 'That silly grin on your face tells me 'that man' has talked you into it.' I was silent. It was true."

There was a lot to do. Flynn wrote, "I decided I would straighten out the question of the amateur politicians at once. I went to the President and told him I did not want the New Deal amateurs to be associated with the National Committee at all in the campaign. The President agreed that all future appointees would first be submitted to me so that I might check with the regular organizations concerned. This worked well in many instances. In many others it did not. The President did not keep his word on many appointments."

Flynn had a reputation at the White House of fighting hard, and directly with the president, to hold Roosevelt to his word. For example, while Flynn was in California during the campaign, he learned that, without party approval, a New Dealer had been nominated to become federal attorney for the southern district of New York, in effect the federal government's district attorney for Manhattan, the Bronx and several other nearby counties. As Flynn recounted, "To put it very mildly, I was upset. I immediately called the President on the telephone and in plain and emphatic language told him what I thought about his action in making this appointment after he had told me he would not do so without consulting me. I told him that I was coming back to New York and that it was up to him to find a new National Chairman. I was so angry that before he had a chance to explain I very rudely hung up the telephone."

Although it took several days, Flynn cooled down and reconciled with the president. He blamed the appointment and others like it, on "the New Dealers who surrounded him [Roosevelt] ... constantly belittling the Democratic organizations and ... continually suggesting names of people who were opposed to the organization."

The party's Washington headquarters was not a happy place. Some staff members were Farley loyalists, and either resigned or were replaced. While Flynn knew the national committeemen from the other states and other top party people, he felt "at a disadvantage ... because while I knew most of the main political leaders, my connections did not go down to the roots of the party." To correct for this, he set off on an ambitious travel itinerary across the country and scheduled many meetings in New York.

The campaign strategy couldn't have been simpler. The president inspected military installations and defense industry sites, focused attention on his presidential responsibilities, and held off on actual campaigning until the last few weeks before the elections. This meant that Flynn, as party chairman, had to meet at least daily with the press, something he was initially not comfortable doing. "One of the most difficult situations I faced was personal," he wrote. " It was my meetings with the newspaper men and women. During my entire political career I had never given out a public statement as coming from me personally. The newspaper men in and around New York knew this and, in most instances, never bothered to call me, since they knew it would be useless. I frankly confess that I had a fear of newspaper men and women."

His first press conference, involving a hundred or so reporters, featured a nervous Flynn seated on a raised dais in a large room at Washington's Mayflower Hotel. Flynn remembered, "Afterward I felt that I had escaped with my life." There followed regular morning and evening conferences, mostly in New York, with Flynn becoming more and more comfortable, "As time went on," he recalled, "I became better acquainted with them and my dislike for press conferences grew less and less. Finally I grew to enjoy the give-and-take of these meetings."

The record shows that Flynn could be effective in bringing the battle to the Republicans. To take one example, the day after Willkie made a strong pitch for labor support, Flynn replied. Using company records, he charged that the Commonwealth and Southern Utilities Corporation, the company Willkie had headed, engaged in "ruthless anti-labor activities including hiring the Pinkerton National Detective Agency to spy on the workers." Willkie fought back, arguing that the detectives were "operation inspectors" and not spies, but Flynn had scored political points.

Organizationally, Flynn divided the country into five zones, taking direct charge of the eastern one and appointing experienced party people to manage the other four. One of his biggest headaches was dealing with cabinet members and other prominent Roosevelt supporters looking for chances to speak and seeking local party sponsorship. They were not always welcome. The most difficult on this score was Secretary of Interior Harold Ickes, with whom, Flynn said, "I had to be brutally frank."

Immediately after the Chicago convention Flynn, and many other Roosevelt supporters, feared defeat. In nominating Wendell Willkie, the Republicans had chosen an attractive candidate. There was considerable opposition across the political spectrum to a third term. Most newspapers and magazines were in Willkie's camp, and the GOP had no trouble raising funds. Global events, however, worked in Roosevelt's favor.

In the spring of 1940 the German army raced across northern Europe. The Sunday before the Republican convention convened in Philadelphia in late June, the headline across the first page of one of the local papers read, "France Signs on Hitler's Terms." German victories undercut support for several isolationist candidates for the Republican nomination, and—to the surprise of almost everyone—the party nominated lawyer-businessman Willkie, an avowed advocate of American aid to the allies. Willkie supported Roosevelt in the transfer of 50 destroyers to Great Britain, Lend Lease, and instituting the draft, as well as many New Deal domestic programs. As Roosevelt said at the time,

Willkie "is showing what patriotic Americans mean by rising above partisanship and rallying to the common cause." Willkie, every bit as much as Roosevelt, was willing to meet Churchill's challenge, "Give us the tools and we will finish the job."

As the campaign progressed, Willkie's chances diminished. Partly it was voters rallying behind the incumbent. But there were also other reasons, as Flynn observed, "Willkie was at his peak of his strength right after his nomination. He lost ground as soon as he began traveling the country ... some of these [Willkie's] speeches were good, but their chief impact was that while he agreed with the President in both foreign and domestic policies, he asked people to believe that he could carry out those policies better than President Roosevelt, who had created them." Flynn, always a believer in the importance of party organization, also attributed Willkie's defeat to "the lack of support given him by the regular Republican organizations."

During the campaign, each camp chose not to go public with damaging personal information. The Democrats knew, as did many others, of Willkie's extra-marital relationship with the literary editor of *The New York Herald Tribune*. In fact, Willkie did little to hide the affair, even holding a press conference in the woman's apartment. At one point Roosevelt raised the question of whether his campaign should leak the story to the press: "We can spread it as a word-of-mouth thing or by some people way down the line." There is no record showing where Flynn stood on Roosevelt's suggestion, but it was never acted upon. The Roosevelt campaign may have been dissuaded from acting by its knowledge that the Willkie campaign could have retaliated by releasing copies of letters written by Wallace to a mystic philosopher that might cause voters to question his judgment.

Roosevelt was re-elected comfortably, although not as decisively as four years earlier. The popular vote was 27,303,945 to 22,347,744 (the most a Republican candidate had ever received while winning or losing). Roosevelt/Wallace carried 38 states, including every large city except Cincinnati. The Democrats continued their post-Reconstruction dominance of the old confederacy. How much longer could the party appeal to both the urban north and the white-only south?

One final word on Willkie, who would give significant support to Roosevelt during the third term. Columnist Walter Lippmann wrote this about him: "Second only to the Battle of Britain, the sudden rise and nomination of Willkie was the decisive event, perhaps providential, which made it possible to rally the free world when it was almost conquered. Under any other leadership but his, the Republican Party in 1940 would have turned its back on Great Britain causing all who resisted Hitler to feel abandoned." Unappreciated by the power brokers in his own party, Willkie died before the next presidential election.

22 ALMOST AMBASSADOR

When Flynn agreed to take over from Farley as national party chairman and run the 1940 campaign, he made it clear to the president that he would serve only through the election. Somehow Roosevelt never got around to finding a replacement, and Flynn spent the next two years traveling the country as party leader. Roosevelt did send a note to Helen Flynn apologizing for taking so much of her husband's time.

The longer Flynn continued as party chairman, the more he became a target of attacks by Republicans and certain journalists. The lead attacker was newspaper publisher Roy Howard. We have already seen how Howard had alienated Flynn by jumping from McKee to La Guardia during the 1933 mayoral campaign. To quote Flynn, "He [Howard] has worked pretty hard to inherit the Hearst mantle of journalistic 'king-maker' in New York and on the national scene. He has never been kindly disposed to those who did not take this pretension seriously. Moreover, where I was concerned he may have had it on his conscience that he had run out on a promise in 1933. In any event, he had had it in for me ever since that occasion."

As discussed earlier, Flynn, the most powerful Democratic boss in New York, and La Guardia, the Republican mayor, were rivals for Roosevelt's patronage and political support. Against Flynn's urgings, Roosevelt remained publicly uncommitted in the 1933 mayoral election, and supported—albeit in a roundabout way—La Guardia's re-elections in 1937 and 1941. La Guardia endorsed Roosevelt in 1936, 1940 and 1944. Behind the scenes, Flynn and La Guardia knew they had to accommodate each other. One example of this was La Guardia, at Flynn's request, saving the jobs of four Bronx patronage holders over the objection of the city's civil service commissioner. Neither the mayor nor the commissioner would back down. Finally, La Guardia fired the commissioner for insubordination. The commissioner, as a way to get back at La Guardia, attacked Flynn, going public with a story the press dubbed "the paving blocks scandal." Howard played up the story, both in New York and nationally. Although the facts vindicate Flynn, there were those, including Senator Patrick Moynihan, who believed he never fully recovered emotionally from the experience.

Here are the facts. The Flynns had a vacation house near Lake Mahopac in Putnam County, New York. When one of Flynn's sisters died in 1937, Flynn inherited her farm in neighboring Carmel. After deciding to sell the Mahopac place and move to the late sister's farm, the Flynns undertook a number of improvements, costing between $35,000 and $40,000. One improvement was to pave the courtyard with Belgian blocks. As the landscape architect was unable to find a local contractor to do the paving work, Flynn suggested to her that she ask the Bronx commissioner of sewers and highways for suggestions. Unbeknownst to Flynn, the commissioner arranged for county employees to pave the courtyard at a total labor cost of under $750. On a visit, Flynn did see the paving workers, but he had no idea they were public employees. When he did learn the truth, in January 1942, he immediately reimbursed the city. He had already paid a bill for delivery of the paving blocks. The commissioner was forced to retire. City and grand jury investigations followed, with extensive press coverage. A fair conclusion is that Flynn was innocent and completely exonerated by the facts.

In late 1942, with the country and the world at war, Roosevelt approached Flynn about a major ambassadorial appointment, minister to Australia—really ambassador, although technically the ambassador to the Court of St. James in London was the sole ambassador to all the countries in the British Commonwealth—and ambassador-at-large to the South Pacific. Roosevelt made a point of asking Flynn to report directly to him on matters outside of routine ministerial duties. The fact that Flynn was Irish Catholic with strong labor union credentials made him a particularly attractive candidate for Australia, given its labor party government and many citizens of Irish descent. Flynn was interested. It was perhaps the only federal job that ever attracted him other than the earlier senate possibility and, after the war, minister (now ambassador) to the Vatican.

On January 8, 1943, Roosevelt announced his appointment of Flynn as minister and ambassador, subject to senate confirmation. Flynn resigned as chairman of the national Democratic Party, national committeeman for New York and leader of the Bronx organization. Here is Flynn on what happened next, "And then the storm broke. My appointment seemed to be the signal to all the men, particularly in the Senate, who had been fighting the President."

The national press, particularly Roy Howard's papers, revived the paving blocks story. Several Republican senators, joined by Democrats who had been subjects of Roosevelt's failed purges in 1938, attacked the nomination. In the Flynn correspondence collection at the Roosevelt Library there are many letters from this period attacking Flynn as much for his religion, politics and urban residence as for any supposed corruption. Roosevelt remained silent. In late January the senate foreign relations committee approved the nomination, but then Flynn withdrew his name stating, "I am unwilling to permit my candidacy to be made the excuse for partisan political debate in the Senate. What happens to me is not important." Historians have criticized Roosevelt for his apparent reluctance to spend political capital to publicly support his own people in difficult situations, the Flynn ambassadorial controversy being an example. Flynn, whatever his own private views, never did. He did take back his positions as Bronx leader and New York national committeeman, and suggested Frank Walker, a long time party operative and Farley's successor as postmaster general, as national party chairman. A year later, another Flynn protégé, Robert Hannegan, commissioner of internal revenue, succeeded Walker.

23 THE ELECTION OF 1944

In 1942, Thomas Dewey, the Manhattan district attorney and respected crime fighter, decided to run for governor of New York on the Republican ticket. Flynn realized that, were he to win, Dewey would be a formidable candidate for president two years later. He also understood that the leading candidate for the Democratic nomination, John Bennett, the state's attorney general, was not a strong standard bearer. Bennett, who had risen through the Brooklyn organization, did, however, have significant support from Jim Farley, Tammany Hall and his home county's party regulars. With Roosevelt's tacit support, Flynn convinced United States Senator James Mead to contest Bennett for the nomination, but Mead entered the race too late. Truth be told, Flynn's support was also a mixed blessing. Papers as far away as *The Chicago Tribune* made reference to "Edward J. (Paving Blocks) Flynn." The Democratic state convention supported Bennett, and the voters, in November, elected Dewey. At their 1944 presidential convention, the Republicans nominated Dewey, as they would again in 1948.

The 1942 congressional elections went badly for the Democrats. In the senate, the Republicans gained nine seats, bringing the Democrats down to a 58-37 majority. In the house, the Democrats lost 45 seats, barely holding on to a nine-seat edge. The recurring Democratic problem of low voter turnout in non-presidential election years was in evidence, with a total vote of 26 million, roughly half what it had been two years before. Wartime employment disruption and the growing number of men and women in military service certainly contributed to the low turnout. As would become more evident in the 1944 presidential election, many southern states did little to encourage servicemen to vote for fear of enfranchising African-Americans.

Come 1944, Flynn and others close to Roosevelt remained confident that the president, should he choose to run, would be reelected to a fourth term. The 1940 election had settled the two-term-limit issue, and the country was not about to change leaders in the middle of a war that was increasingly going well. For Flynn, the big question the election presented was Roosevelt's health. As he noted as early as the fall of 1943, "Signs of failing health in the President were unmistakable ... His appearance was not good and he complained of a cold that he did not seem able to shake. His usual pep and keen interest in things were missing."

In April 1944, the Flynns spent a night at the White House, and for two hours before going to sleep they discussed how ill the president seemed. A few days later, Flynn met again with Roosevelt, "He did not seem to have the same enthusiasm and the same firmness. He seemed to procrastinate and to lack the power to make decisions, and very frequently he showed signs of irritation. This latter factor was particularly unusual, for in my long acquaintance with him, I had never before seen an irritable note."

During the spring and early summer of 1944, Flynn repeatedly urged Roosevelt not to run for a fourth term. "Because of my affection for him, no other course was open to me." Flynn "begged"—his word—Eleanor Roosevelt to convince her husband not to seek reelection. Meanwhile,

Roosevelt's personal doctor, a career navy officer who would soon be promoted to rear admiral, hid from everyone— including, to some degree, the president—his patient's worsening heart condition. Almost everyone close to Roosevelt other than Flynn, from the New Dealers to the party bosses, wanted him to run, and win, again. Roosevelt saw himself as leading the post-war world into an era of permanent peace. At the convention, there was none of the "will he - won't he" drama of four years before. Although several southern delegates tried to create a pro-segregation insurgency, they failed and Roosevelt's renomination on the first ballot was uncontested.

The convention was not without its controversy, however. It had to do with whether Henry Wallace should be renominated for vice president. Unions and the left generally supported Wallace, while the party bosses did not. For the party men, Wallace was too eccentric, unreliable and liberal. Several weeks before the convention Roosevelt turned to Flynn, asking him to take a trip across the country to meet with party leaders and report back on the advisability of Wallace remaining on the ticket.

Flynn was perfect for the assignment. He was liked and respected by the party men and also knew Wallace fairly well. As noted earlier, they had become "very friendly" while Flynn was serving as the United States commissioner to the New York World's Fair and Wallace was secretary of agriculture. Of particular concern was Wallace's probable effect on the ticket's chances in the more heavily populated states. Flynn reported back to Roosevelt that Wallace presented too great a risk.

The next assignment followed from the first. Roosevelt asked Flynn to lead the effort to identify Wallace's successor, and then sell the chosen individual to the party. Flynn set out to find, in his words, the candidate who "would hurt him [Roosevelt] the least." Senator James Byrnes of South Carolina, later to become Truman's secretary of state, was a leading possibility. He was eliminated, to quote Flynn, because "he had been raised a Catholic and had left the Church when he married, and the Catholics wouldn't stand for that; organized labor, too, would not be for him; and, since he came from South Carolina, the question of the Negro vote would be raised." As noted earlier, these same concerns probably would have eliminated him as a presidential candidate in 1940 had Roosevelt decided not to go for a third term. Sam Rayburn of Texas, later to become house speaker, was well-liked by Flynn, but suffered from some of the same civil rights concerns as Byrnes. Others were considered, and Flynn later remembered he "went over every man in the Senate."

Only one fit, Senator Harry Truman of Missouri. Here is Flynn on Truman, "His record as head of the Senate Committee to Investigate the National Defense Program was excellent, his labor votes in the Senate were good; on the other hand, he seemed to represent to some degree the conservatives in the party, he came from a border state, and he had never made any 'racial' remarks." Truman's close ties to the Pendergast machine in Kansas City probably cut both ways. All the known communications among Roosevelt, Flynn and others concerning Truman's qualifications centered on what Truman would bring to the ticket politically, and none as to whether he was the best choice on the merits to succeed Roosevelt as president.

With Roosevelt, nothing was simple. He had committed publicly to an open convention vote for the vice presidential nomination. Several candidates, including Wallace and Byrnes, thought they had Roosevelt's tacit support. Meanwhile, Flynn and the others on Roosevelt's team were working the delegates for Truman. The night before the vice presidential vote, in a proverbial hotel room full of cigar smoke, whiskey and party leaders, Flynn laid down the law—or actually the president's demand—that Truman be selected. As historian David McCullough put it, "Ed Flynn had been in town less than a day and everything had changed." The rest is history. Although Wallace received a significant number of votes on the first ballot, Truman was nominated easily on the second. The following April, Roosevelt would die. One of Flynn's children has a photograph of Truman that the new president gave to his father, with the inscription "My very best to my friend Ed Flynn who helped me run into a lot of trouble."

McCullough told son Richard Flynn years later that his father "was the maker of one of our greatest presidents, Harry S. Truman."

Paris was liberated in August 1944, and the Japanese navy was badly beaten at Leyte Gulf in the Philippines in October. Roosevelt, carefully giving the impression of being in good health, made a vigorous late campaign swing, often riding in an open car, as he did in the pouring rain in New York City. In the election, the Roosevelt/Truman ticket won 36 states and 53.4 percent of the popular vote. It did lose both Hyde Park and Independence, Missouri, the candidates' home towns.

Organized labor came of age in the 1944 election. The American Labor Party (the more moderate part of which became the Liberal Party in New York) was created in 1936 by Sidney Hillman of the Amalgamated Clothing Workers and David Dubinsky of the International Garment Workers. Flynn, although supportive of labor and with solid union connections, was never happy with this development, fearing that a third party would take votes from the Democratic line. It did just that in supporting La Guardia in 1937 and 1941. Roosevelt was always more supportive, believing the new party would move Democrats in a progressive direction. The votes Roosevelt received on the American Labor Party line in 1944 allowed him to carry New York. Hillman became a major force behind the creation of the Congress of Industrial Organizations—C.I.O.—representing assembly line workers ignored by the skilled craft unions that made up the older American Federation of Labor.

24 ROOSEVELT'S FINAL DAYS

Immediately after his reelection in 1944, Roosevelt asked Flynn to undertake a special assignment. The president understood that he would need the cooperation of the Soviet Union to achieve a peaceful world order after the war. He also knew that, in terms of domestic politics, accommodation with the Soviets would generate fierce opposition by anti-communist elements in both political parties. Many Catholics were particularly concerned about the Stalin government's professed atheism and repression of religious expression. Roosevelt's task for Flynn was to undertake an extensive fact-finding mission in the Soviet Union to determine the state of religious freedom and government policy concerning religious education, expression and organization. Flynn was asked to join the American delegation to the famous Yalta conference, where Roosevelt, Stalin and Churchill discussed the post-war world, and then go on to Russia. In selecting Flynn, Roosevelt knew he was choosing someone who shared his belief in the importance of international cooperation as represented by the creation of the United Nations.

Diplomats and party bosses form very different employment pools, but Flynn was an exception. As McCullough noted, Flynn in 1944 was "the most powerful boss in the country and ... in looks and manners bore little resemblance to the usual

picture of a successful Irish politician ... At fifty-two, Flynn
was tall and handsome, with thinning gray hair and gray eyes,
beautifully dressed, well educated, an ardent gardener, a
student of history." McCullough's description fails to include
the fact that Flynn was for several years named on a best-
dressed men's list, although his children believe that the judges
must have passed blindly over their father's loud ties.

The American delegation had an arduous trip to Yalta. First
they crossed the Atlantic by cruiser, with an eight-destroyer
escort guarding against U-boat attack. Next came plane rides
from Malta to one of Yalta's airports, and then a four-hour
mountain drive to the former royal palace where the conference
was held. On the trip, Flynn thought the president looked
"very bad." At the conference, he was impressed with how
Roosevelt could rally "by a supreme effort of will" when
necessary. "But later in his bedroom I was shocked at the toll
that had been taken by his years of labor."

While not participating in the actual negotiations at Yalta,
Flynn did meet with Stalin and Foreign Secretary Molotov,
both of whom pledged their assistance on his Russian trip, as
well as Churchill. Flynn came away from Yalta impressed with
how Harry Hopkins supported Roosevelt: "There was no one
who was more helpful to the President at this time. Hopkins
was able to take the burden of a great deal of detail from the
President."

After the conference Flynn flew to Moscow. He spent a
month traveling in the Soviet Union, inspecting church
practices and educational programs. The more he met with
those involved with religion, education and youth
development, the more he came to question whether he was
getting an accurate picture. As he later wrote, "The whole
situation seemed so complex and so contradictory that it was
difficult to form any definite opinions. Just about the time I

had my mind made up on something, something would occur that would completely change it. They [the Russians] try to be cooperative and pleasant, but sometimes one has a feeling that they, to say the least, are not entirely frank."

Travel was hard, living arrangements were uncomfortable, and it was always cold. Flynn appreciated that an American army officer had given him a pair of fur-lined galoshes and Ambassador Averell Harriman had lent him a long fur coat. Visiting a local market, Flynn was offered five thousand rubles (roughly $1500 at the time) for the overcoat, and he thought he might have been able to bargain for a higher price. Flynn was quite sure, however, that Harriman, heir to a railroad fortune, did not need the money.

Almost half a century after Flynn's Russia trip, John Melby, who as second secretary in the U.S. embassy in Moscow had been assigned to travel with Flynn, recalled, "For me the association with Edward Flynn was pure delight. The public image of a Tammany type of political boss had nothing to do with Ed Flynn. Urbane, worldly, beautifully and comprehensively educated, humorous, a world traveler, he had all the charm and magnetism in the world." At trip's end, Flynn confided in Melby that he expected to be appointed United States minister to the Vatican, and invited Melby to become his deputy.

Flynn never completed a report on his trip. In his words, "It is virtually impossible ... and thoroughly unfair for anyone to come to any positive conclusions about a country as vast as Russia on the basis of the small experience of a month's stay." For the rest of his life, however, Flynn recognized that world peace depended on good relations with the USSR. He was aware of the great suffering the war had caused the Russian people, and how the Soviet "experiment" was in its infancy. Commenting in 1947 about the Soviet expansion in Eastern

Europe, he wrote, "While unquestionably the high-handed methods they (USSR) used in seeking to have friendly governments surrounding them have been wrong, we must realize that it is a very normal reaction for Russia to seek to have sympathetic governments on her borders."

On the trip home from Russia, Flynn stopped in Cairo, Athens, Rome, Paris and London. There were meetings with foreign leaders, embassy dinners and press conferences. In Rome, he met twice with the Pope and held a press conference with 70 reporters. He later informed Eleanor Roosevelt that he had "told His Holiness the church should change their tactics and stop attacking the Soviets." In London, he discussed his trip with Prime Minister Churchill. It was there, on the night of April 12, 1945, that Flynn was awakened and told of Roosevelt's death: "It was as if one of our own family had died." He remembered thinking, "He was as truly a war casualty as any man in uniform who fell in battle." Flynn flew home on the president's plane with Roosevelt's son Elliot, Samuel Rosenman, and financier Bernard Baruch. It was Baruch who once observed, "While everyone professed a willingness to do what the boss—Roosevelt—wanted, the boss did what Ed Flynn wanted."

25 ROOSEVELT IN RETROSPECT

Flying back to the United States after learning of Roosevelt's death, Flynn could think only about the late president and their close friendship and political alliance: "For our friendship through the years had come to be very deep and affectionate. Incidents, small in themselves, but magnified by their multitude, stood out one by one in high relief. But because our relationship was so close and our principal interests were political, it was always impossible to separate personal affairs from political." Of course, with Roosevelt there is always the question of whether he had close friends. Historian Arthur Schlesinger Jr. described him as "glittering, impersonal ... superficially warm, basically cold." His long-time assistant Missy LeHand believed he "was really incapable of a personal friendship with anyone."

Although Roosevelt and Flynn first met in 1918, it was at the 1924 Democratic convention that their friendship really began. Flynn led the Bronx delegation committed to Al Smith. Smith was placed in nomination as "the happy warrior" by Roosevelt, who would also nominate Smith in 1928. During the mid-1920s, Flynn frequently visited Roosevelt at the Fidelity and Deposit Company, where the future president was an officer. Within the political community their friendship was recognized, which is why in 1928, as already noted, "Smith felt I could more easily persuade Roosevelt to run for Governor than he could." Remembering when the newly elected governor asked him to serve as secretary of state, Flynn wrote, "I don't believe I would have accepted but for his great personal persuasiveness. ... This personality always had a great bearing on Roosevelt's political success."

How did Flynn see Roosevelt? "There was no one I have ever known who was more socially agreeable to be with than President Roosevelt. He loved a good story and his own stories were sometimes fantastic. ... Until a few months before his death he was always gentle. He was full of fun and enjoyed everything he did." Flynn also recognized that Roosevelt had "a phenomenal ability to absorb knowledge" and "a prodigious memory for facts." He was able at a moment's notice to talk "intelligently on all sorts of unrelated subjects." And yet Flynn, like others close to Roosevelt, "never saw him read a book ... or a magazine, unless a particular portion was called to his attention." He acquired his information through conversation.

Flynn found Roosevelt to be in charge of his administration: "The fundamental idea in so far as the New Deal was concerned was the President's own." Of course he relied on skilled aides and experts to develop policy, "but it by no means meant that the people who prepared these memos shaped the course of the President's thinking. I have seen him forcibly reject suggestions in which he personally did not believe."

As for Roosevelt's political orientation, "He believed the entire world was trending to the Left and subsequent events proved that he was right. This was a world-wide trend that few people saw as early as he did. But he felt that in order to preserve the capitalist system, much legislation had to be put on the books that was Left of Center." Roosevelt and Flynn shared a progressive and inclusive vision for the Democratic Party both nationally and in New York: pro-union, pro-welfare, pro-civil rights.

To be sure, Flynn recognized that there were some less attractive aspects to Roosevelt's personality, "His two greatest weaknesses, in my opinion, were the bitterness which he engendered within himself and the weakness which he displayed in his inability to be frank and open in many instances in his dealing with people." An example of how Roosevelt's bitterness could "becloud his judgment" was the attempt to pack the Supreme Court. Flynn wrote, "In my opinion, it was his bitterness against members of the Supreme Court when they upset legislation that he thought should have been sustained that caused him to introduce the Court-packing bill. He had a failing which is human, if you look at it in the right way, to 'get back' at the people who opposed him. I don't think that he ever thought the court legislation was good legislation."

In all their years of close association, Flynn "never knew him to fire anyone ... Many men and women he had selected for various offices proved incompetent in their jobs. He should have removed them as quickly as possible, but instead, rather than offend them, he promoted them in as pleasant a way as possible ... He couldn't say 'no' on matters of personnel."

As for two criticisms often made of Roosevelt—that he could be dishonest and disloyal to his allies—Flynn had his own perspective. "I believe Roosevelt told no more untruths than are 'allowed'... The public interest may at times require a man (in Roosevelt's position) to change his mind, to violate a promise, even to shade the truth." As for loyalty, Flynn found "the President was very loyal to me, and I know this to be equally true with others." As many historians have noted, however, and as Flynn himself discovered when he was being considered for the ambassadorship, Roosevelt was loath to spend political capital to support allies under attack. Flynn accepted this as how the game is played.

26 KINDRED SPIRITS

For many historians Eleanor Roosevelt was her husband's conscience, a constant prod for more progressive policies and a political protector on the president's left. Flynn adored Eleanor. as did Helen Flynn, but he saw her as a less powerful influence on her husband than did many others. He wrote, "I believe from my intimate observations covering a long period of years that Mrs. Roosevelt was credited with more influence than she actually had."

According to Flynn, "Undoubtedly she did influence the President in certain matters. However, it was never true that her opinions were the basis for the President's actions. If he thought her opinions were good, he accepted them. If he thought they were bad, he rejected them. Sometimes she was very insistent on putting across a point of view with which the President disagreed. At such time the President would say, 'Now, darling,' and everybody present, including Mrs. Roosevelt, would know the matter was ended." Interestingly, in her memoir Eleanor observed that Franklin may have listened more to Flynn than to other advisors, but Flynn, in the 1950 oral history at Columbia, said, "It was difficult to know how much that was."

If Flynn knew of the complications of the Roosevelt marriage and the president's relationships with other women, he never mentioned it to his children or in anything he wrote. He found both Roosevelts to be highly sociable and never snobbish. They enjoyed hosting dinners in Albany, the White

House and Hyde Park. In Flynn's words, "All types were brought into their social activities. At dinner there might be a member of the Women's Trade Union League sitting next to one of the Old Dutch aristocrats from Albany, and across the table from a group of musicians brought up from the hills of Tennessee."

Did Flynn have a sense of the tension between Eleanor and her mother-in-law? He did tell stories about the latter. Here is one: "The elder Mrs. Roosevelt, who was one of the last of the grande dames, was sitting on the lawn at Hyde Park one day, watching the activities connected with some sort of handiwork that was being given. Turning to me, she asked in her stentorian whisper, 'Where does Eleanor get all these people?'"

When Al Smith assigned him to convince Roosevelt to run for governor in 1928, Flynn tried to recruit Eleanor to help in the effort. Flynn recalled, "It seemed to me that she was anxious that he [Roosevelt] should run, and that she would be happy if he would consent to it." Eleanor refused to help, however, telling Flynn that she had an understanding with Franklin "that she would not interfere in his decision. She would not urge him either to run or not to run."

As governor, Roosevelt, with Flynn as secretary of state and chief patronage dispenser, made a point of building the Democratic Party in the rural areas. Eleanor was always available to visit upstate counties and support the effort. The same was true as to national politics. Flynn recalled about the 1932 presidential campaign, "When it was necessary for her to be with the candidate, she was always there. She accompanied him on parts of his trips and did a great deal of confidential work for him in contacting various people he wished to talk with throughout the country." Flynn credited Eleanor with making "every effort to get as much information as possible and to convey this information to the President, sometimes information he could have obtained in no other way."

It has been said that Eleanor became a popular public figure only in widowhood, and her earlier role as an activist wife was unsettling to many. Flynn would have disagreed with this, at least as related to Democratic politicians. To quote Flynn about the 1940 presidential convention, "Mrs. Roosevelt sat on the platform during all the deliberations ... We also felt that her presence at the convention would do a great deal to keep things in order. She was universally respected by the Democratic leaders. Invariably they were willing to listen to her and to yield to suggestions that she might make. In dealing with these leaders, Mrs. Roosevelt was always fair and understanding, and they admired her intense loyalty to her friends." At Flynn's request, Eleanor became an active advocate for Henry Wallace's nomination for vice president.

After Flynn withdrew from consideration as ambassador in early 1943, Eleanor wrote him expressing her disappointment and complimenting him on his public service. Her letter concludes, "This letter, however, is only to assure you of my personal loyalty and admiration and my hope that through the years we will continue to be good friends."

Later that year, as noted previously, it became obvious to Flynn that Roosevelt was becoming physically weaker and weaker. In early 1944, Flynn urged the president "not to consider it [running for a fourth term]. I spoke with Mrs. Roosevelt and begged her to use whatever influence she had to keep him from running again. I felt that he would never survive his term."

After President Roosevelt's death, the Flynn-Eleanor Roosevelt friendship became even closer. This was partly the result of shared political values. Flynn was sometimes described in the press as "the liberal boss." He believed in civil rights and equal treatment for African-Americans, the legitimacy and value of unions, and the importance of the United Nations in relieving cold-war tensions. He hated the growing red-scare movement that eventually led to Joe McCarthy. He complained to his children about how members of "their group," Irish Catholics, were so prominent in promoting exaggerated anti-communism. On all these subjects, Eleanor and Flynn were in strong agreement. Flynn hoped that Eleanor would follow him in making a Russian trip—something the Soviets had told him they would welcome—but Truman vetoed the idea.

In the years immediately after the war, there were times when Eleanor would defend Flynn, and times when their roles were reversed. In February 1948, in a special election for a Bronx congressional seat, a pro-Wallace American Labor Party candidate defeated the regular Democratic nominee, something that simply didn't happen in Flynn's Bronx. Voter turnout was very low, and in the November general election, the Democrat who had failed in February won overwhelmingly with over 63 percent of the vote.

At least at the time, the February upset was noticed. President Truman asked Eleanor what she thought of Flynn now. In a letter of response to Truman, she replied that the upset made just the point that Flynn had been trying to make to Democratic Party leaders, which was that, on a range of issues from civil rights to controlling military spending in the face of red-scare tactics, the national Democratic Party was failing to provide leadership. To quote from her letter, "I was not much surprised by the results of the vote because in the big, urban centers, even those who are Democrats just do not come out to vote because they are still radical enough to be unhappy about what they feel are certain tendencies they observe in our Administration. Ed Flynn has told you this, I think, on a number of occasions ... The two things bothering the average man most at present are inflation and the fear of another war."

In a three-page letter to Robert Hannegan, Flynn's second successor as national party head, Eleanor argued for more party support concerning fair labor practices, elimination of poll taxes, the appointment of women to important government positions and other progressive actions. When Flynn told Eleanor that, against his advice, Truman was considering selecting Secretary of Agriculture Clinton Anderson to replace Hannegan as party chairman, she wrote Truman: "I could never support Mr. Anderson. I consider him a conservative and I consider that the only chance the Democratic Party has for election in 1948 to be the liberal party." Truman backed down, although he told Eleanor that Flynn's opposition to Anderson had more to do with a patronage battle than ideology.

In early 1948 a movement developed within the Democratic Party to nominate Dwight Eisenhower for president. Eleanor was worried that her son Franklin would join this chorus, and asked him to speak privately with Flynn. They didn't meet, however, until the day after Franklin announced his support for Ike. Flynn made it very clear to Franklin that he thought the young man was making a mistake. He believed that Eisenhower would not run, and, in any case, the Democratic Party leaders resented Franklin trying to play kingmaker, which they saw as their prerogative. Flynn told Franklin, "You're exactly like your father. Louis [Howe] and I had to hold your father back. Sit still now and let it simmer." General George Marshall, by then secretary of state, gave Franklin similar advice. Soon Franklin received a call from Eisenhower himself, disclaiming any interest in the nomination.

Nineteen forty-nine offered Flynn the chance to defend Eleanor Roosevelt, and he rose to the occasion. It had to do with Cardinal Francis Spellman, the Catholic archbishop of New York, and his attacks on Eleanor. Spellman, when a young priest, was described by the bishop of Boston as follows: "Francis epitomized what happens to a bookkeeper when you teach him to read." Appointed archbishop of New York in 1939 by Pius XII in one of his first acts as pope, Spellman would soon also become vicar for the United States armed forces. The press saw him as a "powerhouse" in both local and national politics.

In post-war America, Spellman became the national leader of the church's effort to achieve public funding for parochial schools. Congressman Graham Barden, a conservative southern Democrat, sponsored a bill to provide federal support for public—but only public—schools. Eleanor Roosevelt was a strong voice in support. Spellman was adamantly opposed unless parochial schools were included, calling the pro-Barden bill effort "a craven crusade of religious prejudice against Catholic children." He called Barden "an apostle of bigotry." Eleanor, in her nationally syndicated "My Day" columns, supported the Barden bill and argued that extending public support to parochial schools would violate the constitutional separation of church and state.

Spellman had already earned his reputation as an outspoken anti-communist, railing against "communist condoners" and claiming that "the first loyalty of every American is vigilantly to weed out and counteract Communism." He attacked the Barden bill and Eleanor's support with equal ferocity, accusing the president's widow of "anti-Catholicism" and calling one of her "My Day" columns an example "of discrimination unworthy of an American mother."

A number of public figures spoke out in favor of Eleanor. Although he was convinced it would cost him the 1949 special senate election—against Republican John Foster Dulles, later Eisenhower's secretary of state—Governor Lehman felt he was honor-bound to defend her. He did so, and yet narrowly won the election. Flynn also publicly defended Eleanor, and—as reported by *The Times'* Warren Moscow—he also went further, secretly flying to Rome and getting Pius XII to call Spellman off. In the late summer of 1949, Spellman visited Eleanor at Hyde Park, and then reduced his demand for public funding of parochial schools to non-curricular matters. At Eleanor's request, he also made it known that he would not oppose Lehman in the senate race.

Flynn's daughter Sheila remembers seeing Eleanor at the Flynn's Carmel house and that her parents gave a large cocktail party in her honor in Riverdale. At that party, Eleanor was accompanied by Joseph Lash, her close friend and biographer. Lash later wrote that, correct as she may have been on restricting government aid to public schools, Eleanor did have something of an anti-Catholic bias "so common in people of her background." Her reluctant and unenthusiastic support of Jack Kennedy in 1960 also has been cited as an example of this bias. Aware that she had become something of a lightning rod politically, with strong supporters and equally powerful detractors, Eleanor told President Truman that he should feel free not to reappoint her to the United Nations delegation. Truman would have none of it, insisting on the importance to the country that she continue.

The following quote from Eleanor Roosevelt makes for a fitting conclusion to a chapter on her relationship with Flynn: "Ed Flynn was more of an intellectual than the usual run-of-the-mill city boss. Perhaps that is why he understood the aims and objectives of the New Deal so well and why he made it his business to really understand and study my husband as a human being and as a politician and a statesman. He forgave that occasionally as a politician my husband really let him down. Actually, he was much more forgiving and understanding than I often was because I was a less good politician, and Ed Flynn could see beyond the actions of the moment to the ultimate ends... ."

27 AFTER ROOSEVELT

As was true for many others, Flynn never fully recovered from Roosevelt's death. He later wrote, "Clearly his passing had taken something of towering significance out of life. And those of us who knew him in the intimacy of personal friendship felt that loss most of all." Also, as daughter Sheila remembers, her father, who first suffered an angina attack in 1938, became increasingly aware in the post-war years of the heart problem that would eventually kill him. Always a practicing Catholic, he became somewhat more observant. Nevertheless, in the final eight years of his life, 1945 to 1953, he continued to be a significant player in the politics of the times.

One of Truman's challenges upon becoming president was dealing with the wave of post- war strikes in key industries such as steel, coal and automobile. By early 1946, more than a million workers were on strike, and railroad unions were threatening to join them. Truman needed someone to convince the key railroad union leaders—particularly A.D. Whitney of the 200,000-strong trainmen's union and Alvanley Johnson of the 80,000-member locomotive engineers—to remain on the job. Truman asked Flynn, who had strong pro-union credentials, to intervene. Truman, to the consternation of the railroad companies, had already proposed a generous settlement offer. On May 21, Flynn met with Whitney and

Johnson, and left the meeting thinking he had failed. A few
days later the union leaders accepted Truman's terms.

In the immediate post-war years, the partition of Palestine
and recognition of Israel were the subjects of heated debate
across America. While there was strong support for the
creation and recognition of Israel in both major parties, there
was also opposition. Many current and former state department
officers were opposed, and General George Marshall, Truman's
secretary of state, described recognition as "playing with fire
while having nothing to put it out." Secretary of Defense James
Forrestal agreed with Marshall.

Truman hesitated. Flynn was strongly in favor of
recognition, as was his law partner and best friend Monroe
Goldwater, a prominent leader of several Jewish organizations.
In the spring of 1948 Flynn met with Truman, and advised
him to "give in" on recognition or expect the New York
delegation to oppose his renomination at the July convention.
Frank Goldman, president of B'nai B'rith, convinced Eddie
Jacobson, Truman's former partner in their haberdashery store,
to also make the case for recognition. Goldman told Jacobson
he had to make the effort because "No one, not even Ed Flynn,
could budge the President." In mid-May, 1948, two months
before the presidential convention, Truman ended the suspense
and publicly recognized Israel. Ever since, historians have
debated whether Truman's recognition of Israel was based on
policy and principle or just good politics in an election year.
Clark Clifford, pro-recognition and a close Truman advisor,
later played down the role of politics. He claimed that voters
who strongly supported Israel would have been in Truman's
camp even absent recognition.

Flynn was also a strong supporter of the inclusion of Ulster
in the Republic of Ireland, and saw similarities between the
case for Irish unification and that favoring the creation of Israel.

The front-page banner headline in *The Gaelic American* of November 5, 1949, stated, "Edward J. Flynn Demands Justice for Irish and Jews." The paper went on to report Flynn's comments at a Zionist Organization of America meeting, "The right of national self-determination is denied to Ireland just as it was attempted to be denied to Israel."

Another hot issue in 1948, as it has always been throughout America's history, was civil rights. In February 1948, Truman sent a message to congress calling for an expanded federal role in combating racial discrimination, and making specific reference to lynching. To Flynn, "It was extremely welcome news." At the 1948 Democratic convention in July, however, the majority report of the platform committee, reflecting Truman's wishes, supported a moderate and somewhat vague civil rights plank. The intent was to keep the southern Democrats loyal to the party. While the majority report was being presented to the convention, Minneapolis Mayor Hubert Humphrey, who became vice president years later, was sitting on the rostrum waiting to address delegates in support of a minority platform report with a much stronger civil rights plank. Humphrey's plank called for, among other things, the elimination of the poll tax, fair employment legislation, and desegregation of the armed forces. Flynn, also on the rostrum, asked Humphrey if he could see the minority report. After reading it, he told Humphrey, "Young man, that's just what this party needs."

Flynn put the word out, and Humphrey's report was adopted, although the vote—651 ½ to 582 ½—was close. Humphrey later wrote Flynn, "I shall never forget the help that you extended at the time of the Democratic National Convention on the civil rights issue." All of Mississippi's delegates walked out, as did most of Alabama's and others from the south. Truman, as one would expect of a sitting president, was renominated overwhelmingly on the first ballot. Senator Alben Barkley of Kentucky, like Truman a border state moderate on racial issues, was nominated for vice president.

After the convention, unhappy southern Democrats—"Dixiecrats"—created the States Rights Democratic Party and ran Governor (and later Senator) Strom Thurmond of South Carolina for president. Many observers thought that the Democratic defections—from the right with Thurmond and a second defection from the left with Henry Wallace, running as the candidate of the Progressive Party—would cause Truman to lose to Republican Thomas Dewey. Had that happened, Flynn might have had to share the blame for the Thurmond and Wallace campaigns.

Events, however, proved that Flynn's position was the right course politically as well as morally. Election results confirmed that the loss of southern white support could be countered by gains in the northern African-American community, which was large enough to make a real difference in swing states and had been historically Republican. The New Deal, and the desire to participate in patronage (particularly at the local level), began the movement of African-Americans to the Democratic Party. Roosevelt received 23 percent of their vote in 1932, 68 percent in 1944. Truman got 77 percent in 1948. There is no question but that Flynn's position on civil rights went beyond politics. In 1943, he wrote an impassioned letter to Eleanor Roosevelt tying world peace to the recognition that "all races are equal."

The 1948 presidential election is perhaps most remembered for the photograph of Truman holding an early edition of the *Chicago Tribune* over his head with the banner headline, "Dewey Defeats Truman." In fact, Truman's upset victory was rather easy. He carried 28 states (303 electoral votes, over 24 million voters) to Dewey's 16 (189 electoral votes, under 22 million voters), with Thurmond (four states, 39 electoral votes) and Wallace (no states, no electoral votes) both receiving one million plus votes. It was the fifth consecutive presidential election victory for the Democrats, and the party also recaptured both houses of congress, lost two years before. For many Americans the Democratic Party had become the party of prosperity, just as the GOP had been in the 1920s.

Although Flynn never developed the close personal relationship with Truman that he had with Roosevelt, the two men worked well together. Both were straightforward, honest, willing to speak their minds. They shared senses of humor and succumbed to occasional outbursts of temper. They also were the products of political machines with the bedrock value of loyalty to the organization. Truman, less than a week after his inauguration as vice president in January 1945, attended the funeral of Tom Pendergast, a convicted felon and the longtime boss of Kansas City, to whom he owed his political career. Once, on a White House visit, Flynn's son Patrick was approached by the president. Truman asked the young man whether he knew that the only person in America who refused to take his telephone calls was his father. Apparently the two men had had a falling-out over a federal judicial appointment. With a big smile, Truman told Patrick that, in time, his father would get over it.

28 POLITICS IS LOCAL

Come 1949, Flynn had to deal with a local political firestorm partly of his own making. Four years earlier William O'Dwyer had seemed to Flynn and his fellow bosses an able and honest regular Democrat and worthy successor to Fiorello La Guardia as mayor. A racket-busting district attorney in Brooklyn, O'Dwyer had also served as a brigadier general (in procurement) during the war. His easy mayorial victory in 1945 had brought city hall back within the Democratic fold.

O'Dwyer was re-elected in 1949, only to resign nine months later to become ambassador to Mexico, an appointment made by President Truman at Flynn's urging. The assumption of many at the time was that O'Dwyer's desire to get out of town post-dated the election and was precipitated by growing public awareness of his personal and political ties to Frank Costello and other underworld figures.

Ever observant Warren Moscow of *The Times* had a different take, and the correct one. According to Moscow, O'Dwyer had been reluctant to run for reelection in 1949, perhaps anticipating the possibility of future scandal. "O'Dwyer liked the power that went with the mayoralty," wrote Moscow, "yet he acted as though he feared the spotlight would search out some vulnerable point in his own past."

Privately both Flynn and Brooklyn Democratic boss Frank Kelly shared reservations about O'Dwyer. What should be done? Flynn, the most powerful boss in town, and with the young Tammany leader Carmine DeSapio following his lead, came up with an elegant solution: convince O'Dwyer to run for reelection with the understanding that he would resign early into his second term and accept a federal appointment. There were political benefits statewide for the Democrats in this scenario. To quote Moscow, "And this could have advantage for the Democratic Party. For instance, if O'Dwyer ran and was reelected in 1949 but resigned in 1950 to accept appointment to some high federal post, there would have to be a mayor election for the balance of O'Dwyer's term. And since 1950 was also a gubernatorial election year, the holding of a mayoral election at the same time would help bring out the Democratic vote in New York City and give the Democrats a chance to recapture the governorship, held eight years by Dewey." As an extra incentive, a U.S. Senate seat was also up in 1950.

Moscow had it right. While O'Dwyer was still hesitating about running for a second term, Flynn arranged for him to meet with Truman. The president offered to appoint O'Dwyer ambassador to Mexico, sometime after his reelection. Truman acted with reluctance, O'Dwyer having been part of an attempt to ditch him as the party's presidential candidate in 1948. Flynn convinced Truman, however, that, in Moscow's words, "the razzle-dazzle would help New York Democrats elect a governor." Upon O'Dwyer's resignation in August 1950, Vincent Impellitteri, president of the city council, became mayor for the rest of the year.

At the same time, Flynn, working with Alex Rose of the Liberal Party (successor to the American Labor Party), put together a slate of state and city candidates for the 1950 election. It included a distinguished Italian-American state supreme court (in New York the trial court) judge for mayor, an equally distinguished Irish-Catholic court of appeals (state's highest court) justice—soon to be replaced by an Irish-Catholic congressman—for governor and Herbert Lehman for senator. It looked like a dream ticket.

Dreams can become nightmares. What no one anticipated was that Impellitteri, the temporary mayor and a man of clearly limited ability, would decide to run for a full mayoral term as an independent candidate. In fact, Impellitteri had some advantages. *The Daily News* shortened his name to "Impy," and portrayed him as the little man against the machine. Elements of the underworld, beholden to Tommy "Three Fingers Brown" Luchese, gave open support. Impellitteri was an Italian-American Catholic running against Democratic and Republican Italian-Americans, both of whom happened to be Protestants. Governor Dewey all but endorsed Impellitteri as a way of splitting the Democratic vote. Without hard evidence, the Impellitteri campaign claimed that its candidate had turned down a bribe of a judicial appointment by DeSapio if he would withdraw from the mayoral race. In the election, Impellitteri received 1,161,000 votes to 935,000 for the Democratic candidate. It was the first time since the consolidation of the city in 1898 that the successful mayoral candidate did not have the endorsement of either major party.

Dewey was reelected to a third term as governor although Lehman was returned to the senate. Moscow described the election as a "fiasco" for which Flynn "bore the real responsibility." Impellitteri's election meant that DeSapio and Flynn were cut off from City Hall patronage, although Flynn was still key for federal positions and made sure DeSapio got his share of these, including collector of internal revenue for New York, postmaster of New York and U.S. attorney for the southern district of New York. According to his son Richard, however, Flynn always had reservations about DeSapio because the Tammany leader sought the limelight. Flynn told his son that most people don't like what bosses do and thus they should be careful to operate behind the scenes.

In 1951 a special election was held to fill Impellitteri's former position of city council president. Rudolph Halley, running on the Liberal Party ticket—with two additional minor party endorsements—was elected. Halley, the lead counsel to Senator Estes Kefauver's committee investigating organized crime, was completely unknown in New York before the committee's televised hearings made him a household name. His election was early evidence of the power of television to influence elections, the political machines notwithstanding.

29 THE CURTAIN LOWERS

The 1952 Democratic national convention was the eighth such gathering Flynn had attended as the Bronx party leader and the fifth as national committeeman for New York. One reporter described him as "happy-go-lucky and active, although his doctors had warned him that his heart would give him no further notice before it stopped beating." What kept him in the political arena—obligation or joy of the game? The answer is probably a bit of both.

As early as 1947 Flynn wrote, "For several years past I have seriously considered resigning. The detail work in a county organization no longer has an appeal to me. Financially the job has been expensive. Naturally, I myself contribute to the support of the party. But there is another item ... whenever a member of the organization is in financial difficulty and comes to me for assistance, I normally lend him money. Some of these loans have even been paid back."

But then why continue? "If I resigned, these men [members of the party organization who had long supported him] would be left out in the cold." Flynn recognized that, were he to resign, he could not protect his people. As he put it, "The old principle that an 'ex' in politics is truly an 'ex' is a verity. Once power has been relinquished, it is difficult either to regain it or to exercise authority through others."

Having held the White House for 20 years, Democrats would have had difficulty in 1952 even if General Dwight

Eisenhower weren't heading the Republican ticket. Truman supported Governor Adlai Stevenson of Illinois for the Democratic presidential nomination, although he grew frustrated with Stevenson's early indecision about becoming a candidate. The president had less patience for Senator Estes Kefauver, the other leading possibility, who took to wearing a coonskin cap to remind voters of his country-boy background. Truman called him "Cowfever." A year earlier Flynn had urged Truman to run for reelection, but to no avail.

The New York delegation, with Flynn and DeSapio in firm control, came into the convention supporting Averell Harriman as a favorite son. Harriman, heir to a fortune and with a distinguished record of public service, had never held elective office. He was not considered a serious candidate, and, at the appropriate time, Flynn and DeSapio delivered the New York delegation to Stevenson, assuring him the nomination. Two years later, Harriman, whom Flynn's children considered a close friend of their father, would become DeSapio's successful candidate for governor of New York. In the 1952 presidential election, the Republican ticket of Eisenhower and Nixon easily defeated the Democrats' Stevenson and Sparkman. The Democratic ticket was yet another effort to bridge the party's north-south split, John Sparkman being the segregationist governor of Alabama.

The mayoral election in New York always comes the year after a presidential election. Mayor Impellitteri decided to run in the Democratic primary in 1953, hoping to hold on to City Hall as a full-fledged Democrat. He had the support of the regular party organizations in Queens and Staten Island thanks to the persuasiveness of patronage, and in Brooklyn thanks at least in part to Luchese and organized crime. Flynn and DeSapio, representing not only the Bronx and Manhattan but also the more reform and liberal elements in the party, countered with young Bob Wagner, the Manhattan borough president and son of the senator. It was a good choice. Wagner beat Impellitteri two to one in the primary and was easily elected mayor in November. Flynn, who died in August, did not live to celebrate Wagner's victory.

Wagner's three terms as mayor, 1954 until 1966, coincided with huge changes in the demographics and politics of the city. A loyal Tammany man like his father when first elected, he grew closer to the newly emerging reform wing of the party and away from DeSapio. Eleanor Roosevelt (upset for the rest of her life at DeSapio for supporting Harriman rather than her son Franklin for governor in 1954), Herbert Lehman and other prominent old-time Democrats found themselves supporting progressive candidates—so-called reform Democrats—against the regulars. Flynn's son Richard ran for councilman-at-large in the Bronx as a reformer in 1957 against the choice of his father's old machine. When Wagner ran for a third term in 1961, the joke was that he did so as the candidate to reform his first two terms.

The changing nature of the city and its politics after the war can be seen in what happened to Charles A. Buckley, Flynn's successor as county boss and congressman since 1934 from the northwest Bronx. A former bricklayer who had done well in the construction business, he rose in the house to chair the patronage-rich public works committee. To quote Bronx historian Jill Jonnes, "Flynn was a tall, suave lawyer; Buckley was a short, crude, high school dropout ... [under Buckley] the Irish were most reluctant to relinquish their long-standing hold ...."

Buckley had his day in the sun by offering early and crucial support to Jack Kennedy in his 1960 campaign for the Democratic presidential nomination. Increasingly, however, he appeared out of touch with changing times, and he lost the

Democratic congressional primary in 1964 for the seat he had held for 30 years. The victor was Jonathan Bingham, of a wealthy Connecticut Yankee family, who put together a "reform" coalition of younger and more educated voters with significant Jewish, black and Puerto Rican representation. He also used television effectively. As Jonnes put it, "Boss Buckley had lost touch with the new realities of his own county and the post-war City of New York. His vision was too parochial to see beyond the comfortable sameness of the Bronx clubhouse." Eleanor Roosevelt, Herbert Lehman and Richard Flynn supported Bingham.

Had Flynn lived and continued as the party leader, would things have been different? It's hard to say, but during his entire career he made great efforts to include new and expanding voter groups in the party and its reward system. He reached out to a young Harlem leader, Adam Clayton Powell Jr., and suggested they meet as early as 1943, a year before Powell's election as the state's first black congressman. Four years later he wrote to President Truman urging the appointment of more women. In 1952, Flynn announced that his goal for the Bronx party was to run younger, and implicitly diverse, candidates, and the ideal candidate for an open assembly seat would be no more than 32 years old.

Still, the old patronage system, with the party offering jobs, contracts and assistance in return for votes, was in inevitable decline. Warren Moscow, in a 1947 article in *The Saturday Evening Post* entitled "Political Machines Have Lost Their Grip," observed, "Roosevelt's New Deal was the most formidable enemy the machine system has ever known. Roosevelt's job-creating agencies ... and his social security and unemployment insurance programs were competition as disastrous for the machine's own welfare state as Macy's was to the old corner dry-goods store."

Political machines depended on the steady flow of new immigrants. The restrictive 1924 immigration act was a blow to the system. So, too, were the demographic changes that the big cities experienced beginning in the late 1940s. The southern black diaspora caused the African-American population of New York to double to 800,000 in a decade. The Jones Act of 1917 granted Puerto Ricans U.S. citizenship, but it wasn't until the advent of regular air travel after World War II that the city's population of Puerto Ricans greatly increased (to approximately 500,000 by 1950, with increases of 60,000 a year). At the same time, second- and third- generation children of the earlier immigrants, now often middle class, headed for the suburbs. Samuel Lubell, in *The Future of American Politics*, described one neighborhood he visited in the south Bronx in 1948 as a "dying Jewish neighborhood where the chill of being trapped penetrates everywhere."

The Bronx, like the whole city and other cities, is a place where people come, stay, succeed, fail, leave and come again. Lubell caught this: "The rhythm of the urban frontier, in short, has been the rhythm of the crowd running away from itself with neighborhoods booming and declining in a regular cycle as the masses chased through them. At their heels, as each group struggled upward, could always be felt the pressure of the next climbing group threatening to overtake and engulf them. There was no standing still. Either one climbed or one fell victim to the pursuing slum."

There was something else happening in the Bronx toward the end of Flynn's life that would have a huge effect on many neighborhoods, the construction of several major highways, the most notable being the Cross Bronx Expressway. As early as 1944, Robert Moses, a man of many titles including coordinator of city construction, started planning for a highway connecting the Whitestone and George Washington

Bridges. Constructed between 1948 and 1962, it is seven miles long and six lanes wide. Although minor and relatively easy-to-make route adjustments would have saved neighborhoods in construction's path, Moses would have none of it. Robert Caro, in *The Power Broker*, described how one Bronx community, East Tremont, unsuccessfully fought its destruction.

Where was Flynn on the expressway? Borough President Lyons and most of the county's elected officials were supportive, and we can only assume, as Caro does, that Flynn was as well. In fact, virtually all of the city's leading figures—including, at various times, Mayors O'Dwyer, Impellitteri and Wagner—saw the highway as a way of stimulating business in the Bronx. Jane Jacobs' *The Death and Life of Great American Cities*, with its recognition of the value of local neighborhood cultures, was not published until 1961. Flynn's son Patrick joked that the Cross Bronx Expressway was Moses' attempt to get back at his father.

30 MOTT HAVEN FAREWELL

The Flynns had promised their daughter Sheila that they would take her on a trip to Ireland when she graduated from the Sacred Heart Academy in Noroton, Connecticut. When the time came, mother and daughter tried to call off the expedition, convinced that Ed would find the trip too arduous. He would have none of it. They crossed the Atlantic on the Mauretania, Flynn in a wheelchair. On August 18, 1953, he collapsed in Dublin and died soon after in a local hospital. He was 61. His obituary, with adjoining photograph, appeared the next day in *The New York Times*, beginning by taking up the entire left hand column of the first page. The paper described Flynn as "the last of the old time political leaders in New York City." ED FLYNN DIES IN DUBLIN was the large-type headline across the top of the first page of *The World Telegram and Sun. The New York Post* noted, "The balding, white-haired boss ran his organization with a dignified reserve more characteristic of a corporation president."

Although Flynn had spent most of his adult life as a resident of upscale Riverdale, the family decided to hold his funeral at St. Jerome's in his childhood, and now struggling, neighborhood of Mott Haven in the south Bronx. Helen and Ed had been married there 27 years earlier.

The funeral was really a last hurrah for a disappearing era. Twelve hundred people squeezed into the church, while twice as many stood quietly behind barricades on Alexander Avenue.

The Bronx Democratic district leaders were honorary pallbearers, marching in two lines down the center aisle. Actual pallbearers included Monroe Goldwater and Averell Harriman, who would be elected governor a year later. Mayor Impellitteri and soon to be mayor Bob Wagner were joined by dozens of political and other city figures and veterans of the Roosevelt administration. Helen walked unassisted behind the casket, followed by Sheila and her brother Richard, an army lieutenant. Her other brother, Patrick, a marine lieutenant, was on duty in the Pacific. There was one notable absentee, Cardinal Spellman.

At probate, Flynn's estate was valued at $917,000, or about $8,366,000 in today's dollars. The valuation is net of various standard tax avoidance arrangements that presumably were employed.

EPILOGUE

Eric Goldman, the great historian of 20th century American politics, was hardly a supporter of the political machine, but he recognized that its defenders had in Flynn their best argument. Flynn was proud to be called boss, and was confident of the societal value of his life's work. He saw the political machine as a provider of employment and other assistance to those who had few other sources of support. The party provided an early rung on the ladder into the middle class. Yes, power corrupts, and successful machines often go bad, but he took pride in the ability and integrity of the elected and appointed officeholders in the Bronx. Flynn believed that the corrective to machine corruption is an engaged electorate.

To be sure, the Bronx organization was disciplined and hierarchical. In the final chapter of his book *You're the Boss*, Flynn described a ten-minute meeting in 1945 of the executive committee of the Bronx Democratic Party. The 33 members of the committee unanimously approved, or really ratified, a slate of candidates cleared by Flynn for the coming primary. To quote Flynn, "To begin with, I always see to it that the key party workers have some sort of exempt [non-civil service] positions, if they want them ... the families also—sons, daughters, husbands, wives—of the District Leaders are taken care of in some way or the other." Flynn admitted that, even under civil service, when choosing to hire or promote from a list of qualified candidates, the one with the best political connections has advantages. Perhaps it also should be noted that John Knewitz, the Bronx Republican leader, was the longtime surrogate's court commissioner of records, a sinecure provided by Flynn. It was said that Knewitz made a career out of losing the Bronx.

And yes, Flynn was proud of his organization's ability to win elections. Again, to quote from his book, "For more than a quarter century [this was written in 1947] Bronx County has elected only Democratic county officials. It has become, on percentage, the greatest Democratic county north of the Mason and Dixon line." It was not unusual to achieve an eligible voter turnout of over 85 percent. The community benefitted from the political stability the machine brought to it. According to Patrick Moynihan, "The indispensable elements in this transformation [of the 1900-1940 Bronx] were the extraordinarily powerful and stable urban Democratic Party organizations of the period."

It is certainly true that successful political machines require that their candidates value loyalty to the organization, and potential candidates who appear too independent will not receive machine blessing. Yet Flynn's most important candidates, those at the top of the ticket seeking the most significant jobs, were recognized at the time, and by historians since, as highly qualified.

To take the 1945 Bronx ticket, James J. Lyons was selected to run for a fourth term as borough president and Samuel J. Foley for re-election as district attorney. Both men had excellent reputations. It was said that underworld figures traveling from Westchester County to Manhattan would do so via New Jersey to avoid the risk of arrest in the Bronx. Flynn was also very hesitant to call legislators concerning legislation. One longtime Bronx assemblyman, Christopher McGrath, remembered one call from Flynn over many years, and that was only to delay passage of a bill for a few days. Of course, as another Bronx legislator noted, "You didn't have to be told where Flynn stood, you knew."

Political machines, once so powerful nationally and in their local areas, are much diminished today. Television, social media, outside money, public employee unions, interest groups, civil service, welfare programs, election reforms—all have contributed to their decline. Jim McManus, the fourth generation of his family to serve as Democratic district leader in Manhattan's Hell's Kitchen neighborhood, was quoted recently in *The Times*: "In the old days you could get people jobs, take care of their problems, help with their daily life. But you just can't help anybody any more. You can't even take care of a jury notice."

Progress? Maybe, but let's give the final word to a skeptic, Princeton historian Sean Wilentz: "A lot of people just don't like political parties, and I think that is a terrible thing. Political parties are how things get done ... in American politics. And the more we weaken them, the less gets done." Ed Flynn would have agreed.

BIBLIOGRAPHY

You're the Boss (Viking, 1947), Ed Flynn's part-memoir and part-defense of the political machine, was the source of many of the quotes attributable to him. The book was entirely Flynn's work. His son Richard remembers his father writing it while sitting under a tree on a family vacation in Mexico. Ed later told Richard that he could have "told more" about various individuals, but he didn't want to gossip. Reviewing the book, Warren Moscow found it fair, honest and frank. I agree, and it was my most important primary source.

The Flynn papers at the Franklin D. Roosevelt Presidential Library at Hyde Park (Accession Number 84-5) include considerable incoming and outgoing personal and political correspondence. A reader gets a sense of what a political boss does on a daily basis, with patronage arrangements being at the top of the list. There are letters from national figures, and this book quotes from some of those written by Franklin and Eleanor Roosevelt, Harry Truman and Hubert Humphrey. Letters sent by Flynn reflect a smart boss's practice of not saying—or writing—more than is necessary.

A third primary source is Flynn's oral history with Owen Bombard (Columbia University Oral History Project, March 1, 1950). It is somewhat disappointing, suffering from the interviewer's seeming ill-preparation.

I was able to interview, and follow up with telephone conversations, the three Flynn children (Patrick, since deceased, Richard and Sheila Flynn DeCosse), and meet with Richard's son Ned (also since deceased). Everyone was gracious and helpful. I also had a conversation with Robert Caro, the Moses biographer. The idea for the book originated in a conversation with Professor Eric Goldman, the distinguished historian mentioned earlier, after one of his lectures. I was then an undergraduate, and during the ensuing half century I did nothing with the idea but remember it.

Although there are no biographies of Flynn, there have been several articles on aspects of his political and personal life. The most interesting of these is "Nothing Much to It," a profile by Richard H. Rovere that appeared in *The New Yorker* (September 8, 1945). Also insightful is Raymond Moley's article "The Boss Can't Lose" in *The Saturday Evening Post* (October 5, 1940), written after the author had moved from early Roosevelt advisor to New Deal critic. Flynn was also the subject of a cover story in *Time* (October 17, 1942) and a column by John F. Melby in *Newsday* (April 11, 1990). Melby was the young foreign service officer who accompanied Flynn on the post-Yalta Russia trip. At the Harry S. Truman Presidential Library there is an oral history—Melby interviewed by library director Benedict K. Zobrist on December 8, 1989—that touches on the trip.

The New York Times coverage of both local and national politics during Flynn's time was essential reading for understanding the period, especially articles written over almost two decades by Warren Moscow. His article "How Carmine DeSapio Made Ends Meet" in *New York Magazine* (October 17, 1971) meets the author's high standards. Other relevant articles include "Honest Graft—Playing the Patronage Game" by Martin and Susan Tolchin (*New York Magazine*, March 22, 1971), "How American Politics Went Insane" by Jonathan Rauch (*The Atlantic*, July/August 2011), and a review of *You're the Boss* by anti-machine reformer Richard S. Childs (*Wiley Periodicals*, 1947).

As for other secondary sources, the following includes those of particular relevance to this book.

IRELAND AND IRISH-AMERICA

The Great Hunger: Ireland 1845-1849 by Cecil Woodham-Smith (Harpers, 1962)

The American Irish by Kevin Kenny (Taylor & Francis, 2016)

IRISH-AMERICAN POLITICS

Machine Made: Tammany Hall and the Creation of Modern American Politics by Terry Golway (Liveright, 2014)

Plunkitt of Tammany Hall by William L. Riordan (Popular Classics, 2012)

BRONX

South Bronx Rising: The Rise, Fall, and Resurrection of an American City by Jill Jonnes (Fordham University Press, 2002)

FARLEY

Behind the Ballots: The Personal History of a Politician by James Farley (Harcourt, Brace, 1938)

Jim Farley's Story: The Roosevelt Years by James Farley (McGraw-Hill, 1948)

Citizen Coke: The Making of Coca-Cola Capitalism by Barton J. Elmore (W.W.Norton, 2015)

ELEANOR ROOSEVELT

On My Own by Eleanor Roosevelt (Harper & Brothers, 1958)

Eleanor: The Years Alone by Joseph P. Lash (W.W. Norton, 1972)

Eleanor Roosevelt, Volume 3: The War Years and After, 1939-1962 by Blanche Wiesen Cook (Viking 2016)

LA GUARDIA

Fiorello H. LaGuardia and the Making of Modern New York by Thomas Kessner (McGraw-Hill, 1994)

When LaGuardia Was Mayor by August Heckscher with Phyllis Robinson (W.W. Norton, 1978)

City of Ambition: FDR, LaGuardia and the Making of Modern New York by Mason B. Williams (W.W. Norton, 2013)

FRANKLIN ROOSEVELT

FDR: The New York Years by Kenneth S. Davis (Random House, 1985)

Roosevelt: The Party Leader by Sean J. Savase (University Press of Kentucky, 1991)

FDR 1882-1945: A Centenary Remembrance by Joseph Alsop (Viking, 1982)

Kennedy and Roosevelt by Michael Beschloss (W.W. Norton, 1986)

Traitor to his Class: The Privileged Life and Radical Presidency of Franklin Delano Roosevelt by H.W. Brands (Doubleday, 2008)

No End Save Victory: How FDR Led the Nation into War by David Kaiser (Basic Books, 2014)

Franklin and Winston: An Intimate Portrait of an Epic Friendship by Jon Meacham (Random House, 2003)

1944: FDR and the Year that Changed History by Jay Winik (Simon & Schuster, 2015)

Roosevelt and Stalin by Susan Butler (Knopf, 2015)

Roosevelt: The Soldier of Freedom 1940-1945 by James MacGregor Burns (Harcourt, Brace Jovanovich, 1970)

1940: FDR, Willkie, Lindbergh, Hitler–the Election amid the Storm by Susan Dunn (Yale University Press, 2013)

Franklin D. Roosevelt: A Rendezvous with Destiny by Fred Freidal (Little Brown, 1990)

No Ordinary Time by Doris Kearns Goodwin (Simon & Schuster, 1994)

Franklin D. Roosevelt: A Political Life by Robert Dallek (Viking, 2017)

His Final Battle: The Last Months of Franklin Roosevelt by Joseph Lelyveld (Knopf, 2016) (also see Lynne Olson's brilliant review, *The New York Times* September 20, 2016)

OTHER

Boss Tweed: The Rise and Fall of the Corrupt Pol Who Conceived the Soul of Modern New York by Kenneth D. Ackerman (Carroll & Graf, 2005)

Herbert H. Lehman and His Era by Alan Nevins (Charles Scribner & Sons, 1963)

The Encyclopedia of New York City edited by Kenneth T. Jackson (Yale University Press & New York Historical Society, 1995)

What Have You Done for Me Lately?: The Ins and Outs of New York City Politics by Warren Moscow (Prentice-Hall, 1967)

The Last of the Big Time Bosses: The Life and Times of Carmine DeSapio and the Rise and Fall of Tammany Hall by Warren Moscow (Stein and Day, 1971)

The Impeachment of Governor Sulzer: A Forgotten Story of American Politics by Matthew L. Lifflander (State University of New York Press, 2011)

Tip O'Neill and the Democratic Century by John Aloysius Farrell (Little, Brown 2001)

To the Victor: Political Patronage From the Clubhouse to the White House by Martin and Susan Tolchin (Random House, 1971)

The Politicians & the Egalitarians: The Hidden History of American Politics by Sean Wilentz (W.W. Norton, 2016)

Five Days in Philadelphia: 1940, Wendell Willkie, and the Political Convention that Freed FDR to Win World War II by Charles Peters (Public Affairs, 2005)

The Patriarch: The Remarkable Life and Turbulent Times of Joseph P. Kennedy by David Nasaw (Penguin, 2012)

The Power Broker: A Biography of John M. Bailey Modern Political Boss by Joseph I. Lieberman (Houghton Mifflin, 1966)

Newsmaker: Roy W. Howard, The Mastermind Behind the Scripps-Howard News Empire From the Gilded Age to the Atomic Age by Patricia Beard (Bowman & Littlefield, 2016)

1946: The Making of the Modern World by Victor Sebestyen (Pantheon, 2011)

Truman by David McCullough (Simon & Schuster, 1992)

Lost Warrior: Al Smith and the Fall of Tammany Hall by Kevin C. Murphy (Privately published, copyright 2002-2013)

The Power Broker: Robert Moses and the Fall of New York by Robert A. Caro (Knopf, 1994)

FDR's Quiet Confidant: The Autobiography of Frank C. Walker edited by Robert H. Ferrell (University Press of Colorado, 1997)

Baruch, My Own Story by Bernard Baruch (Hold, 1957)

The Future of American Politics by Samuel Lubell (Torchbooks, 1967)

Anxious Decades: America in Prosperity and Depression 1920-1941 by Michael Parrish (W.W. Norton, 1992)